Preparing Ourselves
to hear
GOD'S VOICE

CHARLES W. MORRIS

Copyright © 2019 Charles W Morris
All rights reserved.
ISBN: 978-1-0999-9002-1

DEDICATION

I dedicate this book to you, the reader, and it is my prayer that you may learn and grow in the intimate knowledge of our Lord Jesus Christ. I pray that your walk with Him will never waiver or cease as you experience a deeper and more intimate love for the King of Glory. May each day reveal more kingdom principles of communication in hearing His voice. May your days with our Lord Jesus Christ be intoxicating like a sweet wine as He and the Father speak over you and you respond in obedience.

CONTENTS

Acknowledgments:	vii
1. Introduction:	1
2. The voices that compete for our attention:	7
3. Desiring to hear God's voice:	25
4. We are created for God's pleasure:	34
5. Be ready to listen, for God is speaking:	45
6. Why do we want to hear from God?	59
7. The joy of experiencing God's voice:	75
8. Getting ourselves spiritually ready; The willing heart:	83
9. Developing spiritual ears to hear:	96
10. Keys to unlocking the treasure of God's voice:	111
11. Things to remember as you seek to hear:	125

ACKNOWLEDGMENTS

I cannot even begin to express the gratitude I have for all who assisted me in making this book possible. My friends encouraged me along the way to write, even when I doubted the value of another book on the topic of hearing God. When it looked like I would not finish this work, they were there, nudging me to continue, which gave me the drive to finish. However, more than anything, I want to give praise and glory to my Lord and Savior Jesus Christ, who guides me, protects me, and sustains me.

I want to thank my dear friend and fellow minister of the gospel, Artur Mironichenko, who, after reading my manuscript, recommended that I add a chapter about the joy of hearing God's voice. He corroborated with me by assisting in writing chapter 7, The Joy of Experiencing God's Voice. Thank you, Artur and Alvena, for your loving service to humanity in advancing the Kingdom of God.

1

INTRODUCTION

So, you want to hear the voice of God? The answer, of course, would be "yes," or you would not have gotten this book to read. Our time is precious; therefore, we want to make the best use of it. We need to spend our time reading Kingdom truths that will result in making us Christ-like in word, deed, and thought. Please, don't get impatient in reading this book and skip chapters. Many will want to go directly to my second book, where we start giving the 15 different ways to hear God's voice. However, I feel it is essential to read the foundational truths in this book first to better identify, evaluate and heed the warnings of hearing voices that are not from God and for laying the right foundations for a life of daily hearing the voice of God. This book will prepare us to hear from the Father and teach us how to get our hearts and mind ready to listen, receive, and obey what the Father is saying. The Bible tells us that we need to hear and to do.

> *James 2:17-18 ESV So also faith by itself, if it does not have works, is dead. (18) But someone will say, "You have faith and I have works." Show me your faith apart from your works, and I will show you my faith by my works.*

> *James 1:22-25 ESV But be doers of the word, and not hearers only, deceiving yourselves. (23) For if anyone*

is a hearer of the word and not a doer, he is like a man who looks intently at his natural face in a mirror. (24) For he looks at himself and goes away and at once forgets what he was like. (25) But the one who looks into the perfect law, the law of liberty, and perseveres, being no hearer who forgets but a doer who acts, he will be blessed in his doing.

It goes without saying that hearing the voice of the Lord should be a primary Christian discipline. Knowing God's voice is a discipline that is a practical and straightforward part of our faith, instead of the current misconception of being mystical and weird. It is a privilege and joy to be able to say that we can and should hear God's voice.

Having had over 40 years of experience in learning how to hear God's voice, this author must say that understanding the sound of the Father has become easier over the years. I also say that in these last days in which we are living, hearing God is even more critical than ever. Training our ears to listen to the Father and not to the other voices that scream for attention is a lifetime goal. This training to hear from God does not mean that we will get it right every time. By faith, we should assume that we are hearing God's voice. If we are right 75% of the time, is that not better than never attempting to tune our ears to His voice and be wrong 100% of the time?

When it seems like we need an answer from the Father the most, those are the times we struggle to hear His voice the clearest. It is a fact that sometimes we will strive to listen to the sound of God, especially when we seem to need it the most. Then other times, when we think we are hearing God with surety, we find out that we were mistaken and were listening to the other voices.

There are countless testimonies from people where after hearing from the Lord, their lives changed forever. Apart from being born again, we should remain confident that nothing is more life transformational as getting a daily personal word from the Lord. When convinced that we have received a fresh word from the Lord, it changes how we view all our circumstances, trials, temptations, afflictions, and decision making.

My prayer for those who read this book is that we will understand that we all can hear the Father's voice and begin to practice what we have learned. Because of the promises of God's Word, we know that our heavenly Father speaks to all His children. The question is not, "Is the Father speaking to us today?" The real problem is, "Do we have ears to hear what the Father is saying to us today?"

> *Hebrews 4:7 ESV again he appoints a certain day, "Today," saying through David so long afterward, in the words already quoted, "Today, if you hear his voice, do not harden your hearts."*

There are hundreds of Scriptures from the Word of God about hearing God's voice. I have entered many of those Scriptures within this study to validate the necessity and create an expectation of hearing God's voice. When I write my books, the editors always want me to leave the full quoted Scriptures out and only place a Scriptural address for the reader to research on his or her own. I can't entirely agree with the editors; therefore, I put the Scriptures in full into the text for the reader to see and read. The Bible says that faith comes by hearing and hearing by the Word. The only thing important in this entire book is the Word of God, which I posted for all to read. So, take the time to read and reread the Scriptures given.

It should be relevant to all of us that we use the Word of God to confirm and interpret the Word of God. The Bible is our highest level of authority and is the final Word on doctrine and correction. Therefore, this author does not apologize for filling the pages of this book with the Word of God. Let the Word of God interpret the Word of God.

MEANINGFUL COMMUNICATION:

Look around you, and you will see that everyone has a phone attached somewhere on their person. There was a time in my life when people only spoke on the phone when at home and then only in times of an emergency or for gathering information about someone who was sick. Now phones are everywhere. We see people talking on their phones in restaurants, in their cars, in classrooms, and yes, even in bathrooms. People want to be in fellowship with someone but loosely connected. I used the term "loosely" because many times, it is communication without any commitment or a real relationship. For the most part, it doesn't cost us anything emotionally, mentally, or relationally to stay on the phone with people. I am sure you have already experienced the fact that some folks will continue to talk until they find something worthwhile to say. However, not all communication has to be fruitless.

Hearing the voice of the Father is by far the most meaningful communication we will ever receive; therefore, it is of the utmost importance when we listen to a sound that we recognize who it is that's speaking. Many of us have had the unfortunate experience of committing to something with full confidence that we heard the voice of God, only to find out later that we had been listening to "other voices." These learning experiences usually cost us more than we had hoped to pay.

When we talk about hearing the voice of the Father, we need to know there are other voices in competition for our attention. In fact, throughout our childhood, we were conditioned to listen to other voices instead of the voice of God. This is even more true today than when I was in school.

When I was in school in Virginia, we had prayer each morning as class began. Once a week, someone would come into the classroom, give out New Testaments, and give a short Bible study. Since the government has outlawed the voice of God in public schools, the students are then unknowingly conditioned to listen to other sounds.

As believers, we must train our ears to hear the Father's voice. One of the biggest problems is NOT the hearing of sounds, but distinguishing which voice is speaking. To listen and attune to the voice of the Father, we need to shut out or silence the other voices that are screaming for our attention.

What is the source of the other voices which bombard our soul, both in our waking and sleeping hours? Yes, we have voices speaking to us during our sleeping hours also. This state of mind is known as our "dream state." Believers are warned in the Word of God to be careful how we hear and what we hear. The Word of God teaches us that words carry the power of life or death and blessing or cursing. Therefore, warning Christians to take heed and pay attention to what they hear should be a priority for spiritual leaders.

> *Mark 4:23-24 ESV If anyone has ears to hear, let him hear." (24) And he said to them, "Pay attention to*

what you hear: with the measure you use, it will be measured to you, and still more will be added to you.

Luke 8:18 ESV Take care then how you hear, for to the one who has, more will be given, and from the one who has not, even what he thinks that he has will be taken away."

Hebrews 2:1 ESV Therefore we must pay much closer attention to what we have heard, lest we drift away from it.

2

THE VOICES THAT COMPETE FOR OUR ATTENTION

As believers, we know we need to take heed of that which is spoken and heard. Therefore, it would stand to reason that we need to know from where the different voices originate. We also need to be equipped to discern one voice from another. There are five different voices which barter for our attention. As we look at these voices, I am sure you can recognize which of the five voices that seems to have the most apparent avenue to your ears, heart, and decision making.

THE VOICE WITHIN US:

The first voice that screams at us is *our voice*. Our voice will battle against our spirit-man. The battle will contain the lust of the flesh, the lust of the eyes, and the pride of life. This is the lustful and selfish desiring voice in our soul that screams "I will have it my way, what I want and when I want it." There were times when we felt sure we had heard God's voice in critical decision-making time when, in reality, we acted on something that our flesh strongly desired. We may find ourselves already emotionally and mentally tied to an item or decision before we start praying about it. Then when we begin our prayer time about it, deep inside our mind is already made up. That emotional and mental tie has already convinced us that we can't live without it. In this position, it will be nearly impossible to hear God's voice on the subject. Some will go ahead and give God credit or blame by confessing that they prayed about it and feel God's leadership in doing or getting what they desired.

In earlier years, having a new vehicle may have attracted our attention. It grabbed my attention every time my car hit three years old. Let's suppose that as soon as we paid off our current car, we would conveniently get a "word from the Lord" to trade that used car in for a new one. Of course, we could justify such a decision on the merit that a new vehicle is more trustworthy and has options that our current "older" car lacks. In reflection, many of us can say that this was not God telling us to go in debt for another five or six years for a new vehicle, but our desire for an upgrade. We might have been operating in the lust of the eyes that dictated our thought process and therefore corrupted our decision-making long before we started praying about it. Many of us can genuinely thank God for our patient spouse, who, over the years, stood firmly by, even in our crazy decisions that we blamed on God's leadership. Since we claimed that we "got a word from the Lord" to purchase that which we desired, it was easier to blame God for our lust of the flesh and passion of the eyes. Ouch!

We can all confuse the authentic voice and will of the Father with our desires. How do we overcome this? As the Apostle Paul taught, we need to learn to die daily and be content in whatever state we find ourselves.

> *1 Corinthians 15:31 ESV I protest, brothers, by my pride in you, which I have in Christ Jesus our Lord, I die every day!*

PREPARING OURSELVES TO HEAR GOD'S VOICE

Philippians 4:11 ASV Not that I speak in respect of want: for I have learned, in whatsoever state I am, therein to be content.

The TV commercials and computer ads are a great pull on our psyche to fulfill the lust of the flesh. How many times have we gotten up from our supper meal feeling full and satisfied, turn on our TV, and after 30 minutes of commercials of food from pizza to hamburgers return to the kitchen for a snack? The voices of the world start becoming our voice, and we talk ourselves into being hungry. Just look around you; we are an obese nation. Whose voices are we listening to that drives our poor eating habits? How did we buy into the whole mindset of the "comfort food" option? If we depressed, rejected, misunderstood, lonely, bored, and a multitude of other emotions, it is okay to grab our comfort food. Whatever happened to prayer and reading the Word when we feel these emotions?

We need to be a people who walk in the Spirit daily so that we do not fulfill the words and deeds of the flesh. The voice within us is our own conscious or subconscious thought process. Listening to our sound is saying that we are speaking to ourselves. This voice is usually from a lustful heart seeking to satisfy a personal desire while looking for spiritual affirmation. By prefacing our decisions with a statement that we received a word from God, we are attempting to place validation into our decision making. It is like saying, "God agrees with me," to our bad decisions.

It is hard to fight against our voice. The driving force behind our sound is the lust of the heart and flesh, and the pride of life. People tell me they have to follow their hearts in their decision making. The Scriptures tell us that we cannot trust our hearts. For this reason, the Scriptures tell us that we need to die to our self, daily. To die to self means to yield up our desires for the will and ways of our heavenly Father. If we walk in the Spirit, we will not satisfy the lusts of the flesh.

> *Jeremiah 17:9 ESV The heart is deceitful above all things, and desperately sick; who can understand it?*
>
> *1 John 2:16 ESV For all that is in the world—the desires of the flesh and the desires of the eyes and pride of life—is not from the Father but is from the world.*
>
> *Galatians 5:16-17 ESV But I say, walk by the Spirit, and you will not gratify the desires of the flesh. (17) For the desires of the flesh are against the Spirit, and the desires of the Spirit are against the flesh, for these are opposed to each other, to keep you from doing the things you want to do.*
>
> *Jeremiah 17:9-10 ESV The heart is deceitful above all things, and desperately sick; who can understand it? (10) "I the LORD search the heart and test the mind, to give every man according to his ways, according to the fruit of his deeds."*
>
> *James 1:13-15 ESV Let no one say when he is tempted, "I am being tempted by God," for God cannot be tempted with evil, and he himself tempts no one. (14) But each person is tempted when he is lured and enticed by his own desire. (15) Then desire when it has conceived gives birth to sin, and sin when it is fully grown brings forth death.*

Mark 7:18-23 ESV And he said to them, "Then are you also without understanding? Do you not see that whatever goes into a person from outside cannot defile him, (19) since it enters not his heart but his stomach, and is expelled?" (Thus he declared all foods clean.) (20) And he said, "What comes out of a person is what defiles him. (21) For from within, out of the heart of man, come evil thoughts, sexual immorality, theft, murder, adultery, (22) coveting, wickedness, deceit, sensuality, envy, slander, pride, foolishness. (23) All these evil things come from within, and they defile a person."

THE VOICE OF THE WORLD:

Now that we have covered the danger of listening to *our voice*, I will move to the next sound that competes for our attention. The second kind of familiar voice we battle with includes other people. We will call this *the voice of the world*. These voices include the current opinions and lusts of others that try to change us. These voices also include all of our memories from our past. Is it not surprising that we seem to remember our failures more than our victories. Likewise, it is the voice of our faults, loses, and failures that scream for our attention.

The world's voice would include everything from people, such as National and State leaders, friends, family members, teachers, and co-workers, to our personal experiences that do not align with the Word and Character of God. The voices of the world include fallen lost humanity and the corrupt system in which they operate. These voices blast us with messages of rejection, rebellion, selfishness, and sensual desires. TV ads with slogans like "Have it your way," "If it feels good, do it," "Get all that you deserve," and "Grab life's gusto," are some of the voices that scream at us to satisfy our flesh, and our emotional and mental cravings, no matter the cost to ourselves or others.

> *1 John 2:15-17 ESV Do not love the world or the things in the world. If anyone loves the world, the love of the Father is not in him. (16) For all that is in the world—the desires of the flesh and the desires of the eyes and pride of life—is not from the Father but is from the world. (17) And the world is passing away along with its desires, but whoever does the will of God abides forever.*

We all have been taught something or given an opinion about something that is outright hostile to God's character and His Word. These seemingly practical ideas corrupt God's Word that is in us like adding yeast to bread dough. We have been commanded to war against these words and bring them into captivity to our Lord Jesus Christ.

> *2 Corinthians 10:3-5 ESV For though we walk in the flesh, we are not waging war according to the flesh. (4) For the weapons of our warfare are not of the flesh but have divine power to destroy strongholds. (5) We destroy arguments and every lofty opinion raised against the knowledge of God, and take every thought captive to obey Christ,*

Having been a Pastor for over forty years, I have had many opportunities to see and hear the abuse of people using "God told me" for their decision-making process. In my personal pastoral experiences, the most common misuse of "God told me," has been in the area of a person's participation in ungodly relationships. The Bible warns and forbids believers against adultery, fornication, and all other forms of sexual perversion.

The Bible tells us not to be unevenly yoked or tied in close relationships or marriage with the ungodly. Even with all the Biblical warnings, I frequently get the excuse from people that God told them to date or marry such and such person, and that once married, they would change for the good. Another statement I get from people participating in inappropriate relationships is "God loves me, and He understands my position." The world screams to us that it is okay to do anything we want to do, with anyone we want to do it with, and no one has the right to judge us, because God loves us, understands us, and has given us a special dispensation of grace to sin.

> *2 Corinthians 6:14 ESV Do not be unequally yoked with unbelievers. For what partnership has righteousness with lawlessness? Or what fellowship has light with darkness?*

> *1 Corinthians 6:9-11 ESV Or do you not know that the unrighteous will not inherit the kingdom of God? Do not be deceived: neither the sexually immoral, nor idolaters, nor adulterers, nor men who practice homosexuality, (10) nor thieves, nor the greedy, nor drunkards, nor revilers, nor swindlers will inherit the kingdom of God. (11) And such were some of you. But you were washed, you were sanctified, you were justified in the name of the Lord Jesus Christ and by the Spirit of our God.*

> *1 Corinthians 6:18-20 ESV Flee from sexual*

immorality. Every other sin a person commits is outside the body, but the sexually immoral person sins against his own body. (19) Or do you not know that your body is a temple of the Holy Spirit within you, whom you have from God? You are not your own, (20) for you were bought with a price. So glorify God in your body.

The counsel for these types of important life decisions is a no brainer. When the Father speaks, He will never violate His Word or the nature of His Character. In forty-plus years of ministry, only one person whom I counseled with, who was involved in an unbiblical relationship, was convicted, convinced, and changed by the Word of God. This man heard God's Word, turned against the voices of the world, including his friends, and did the righteous thing. All the others who received counsel from the Word of God had convinced themselves they had been given a "special Word from the Lord," which superseded God's written Word to live in sin.

Someone can become so emotionally, mentally, and physically bound to a person that their mind and heart becomes fixed and hardened. Regardless of what the Scriptures say, these individuals convince themselves they are okay with God because they "received a word from God." The word they received violates God's written Word and God's character, however, their mind is made up that they are right. The Bible warns us to be careful as to what we hear or listen. It will take discipline, time, and effort to distinguish the voice of the Father from the other sounds. Over time we will recognize the Father's voice by the Word and Character of the message. One of my favorite sayings, which I use in all of my writings, is this: "You will always know the root by the fruit." If our Lord Jesus Christ is the root of a person's life, then that person will bear the fruit of righteousness. However, if you have lousy fruit or no fruit, then the root is wrong. This wrong fruit means they may confess the Lord Jesus Christ with their lips, but their heart is far from Him.

> *Mark 4:24-25 ESV   And he said to them, "Pay attention to what you hear: with the measure you use, it will be measured to you, and still more will be added to you. (25) For to the one who has, more will be given, and from the one who has not, even what he has will be taken away."*

> *2 Corinthians 10:4-7 ESV (4) For the weapons of our warfare are not of the flesh but have divine power to destroy strongholds. (5) We destroy arguments and every lofty opinion raised against the knowledge of God, and take every thought captive to obey Christ, (6) being ready to punish every disobedience, when your obedience is complete. (7) Look at what is before your eyes. If anyone is confident that he is Christ's, let him remind himself that just as he is Christ's, so also are we.*

> *1 John 2:15-17 ESV   Do not love the world or the things in the world. If anyone loves the world, the love of the Father is not in him. (16) For all that is in the world—the desires of the flesh and the desires of the eyes and pride of life—is not from the Father but is from the world. (17) And the world is passing away along with its desires, but whoever does the will of God abides forever.*

> *1 John 4:4-5 ESV   Little children, you are from God*

and have overcome them, for he who is in you is greater than he who is in the world. (5) They are from the world; therefore they speak from the world, and the world listens to them.

THE VOICE OF LOST RELIGIOUS LEADERS:

We looked at the dangers of *our voice* and *the voice of the world,* both of which compete to keep us from hearing God's voice. The third set of sounds come from a group within the church, and we typically would not consider them as a bad influence. These voices come from *lost religious leaders.* It would be foolish of us to think that everyone standing in the pulpit is genuinely born again or walks with God. It would be equally silly for us to believe that every deacon, every Sunday School teacher, and every Church Board leader has experienced salvation. These lost religious leaders consist of those who heap upon us religious laws, traditions of men, and personal pet-peeves. They act and speak as though they have more authority and wisdom than the Word of God. As an example, a Bible verse frequently misused among believers has been John 10:10.

In this Bible verse, our Lord Jesus Christ was warning us about the lost religious leaders who attempt to enter the kingdom of God by another means other than through our Lord Jesus Christ. This John 10:10 verse has been used by many as a reference to Satan and his demons. However, when reading the Gospel of John Chapters 9 and 10 in context, we find that instead of Jesus speaking about demons, our Lord was referring to lost religious leaders. It is the lost religious leaders who come to steal, kill, and destroy. These corrupt leaders carry with them traditions and doctrines of men, which make the Word of God of no effect and powerless in our lives. It is these lost religious leaders that attempt to deceive the multitudes that someone can be right with God and enter into heaven without going through the Lord Jesus Christ.

> *Mark 7:13 ESV thus making void the word of God by your tradition that you have handed down. And many such things you do."*

I shared this with many Pastors over the years. I had one Pastor tell me that he knew I was right concerning the interpretation and context of Jn.10:10. However, he wasn't going to change because of saying that Satan comes to kill, steal, and destroy makes for "good preaching" to stir up the listeners. All the sincere people listening to this preacher are being led astray by him falsely dividing the Word of truth willingly.

> *John 10:1 ESV "Truly, truly, I say to you, he who does not enter the sheepfold by the door but climbs in by another way, that man is a thief and a robber.*

> *John 10:5-8 ESV A stranger they will not follow, but they will flee from him, for they do not know the voice of strangers." (6) This figure of speech Jesus used with them, but they did not understand what he was saying to them. (7) So Jesus again said to them, "Truly, truly, I say to you, I am the door of the sheep. (8) All who came before me are thieves and robbers, but the sheep did not listen to them.*

> *John 10:10 ESV The thief comes only to steal and kill and destroy. I came that they may have life and have it abundantly.*

> *Mark 7:6-8 ESV And he said to them, "Well did Isaiah prophesy of you hypocrites, as it is written, "'This people honors me with their lips, but their heart is far from me; (7) in vain do they worship me, teaching as doctrines the commandments of men.' (8) You leave the commandment of God and hold to the tradition of men."*

> *Colossians 2:22-23 ESV (referring to things that all perish as they are used) — according to human precepts and teachings? (23) These have indeed an appearance of wisdom in promoting self-made religion and asceticism and severity to the body, but they are of no value in stopping the indulgence of the flesh.*

THE VOICE OF THE ENEMY:

So far, we looked at the dangers of *our voice*, the *voice of the world*, and the *voice of lost religious leaders*. All of these compete to keep us from hearing God's voice. The fourth voice which we need to be aware of comes from the enemy. These voices would include **all demonic forces**. The enemy of God's children does not want us to hear from our Lord Jesus Christ and Heavenly Father. The enemy doesn't want us to receive God's voice through His written Word.

In extreme cases, we watch a news story of someone who just committed murder or some other horrible crime against humanity, and these criminals tell the police that God told them to do it. We know our Heavenly Father would never tell someone to commit these terrible acts against people. These misled souls were listening to the voice of the God of this world. The enemy comes as an angel of light deceiving with lies from hell. The enemy will attempt to discourage us as we seek the Lord and seek to walk in the ways of God's righteousness.

> *1 Peter 5:8 ESV Be sober-minded; be watchful. Your adversary the devil prowls around like a roaring lion, seeking someone to devour.*
>
> *2 Corinthians 2:11 ESV so that we would not be outwitted by Satan; for we are not ignorant of his designs.*
>
> *2 Corinthians 11:3-4 ESV But I am afraid that as the serpent deceived Eve by his cunning, your thoughts will be led astray from a sincere and pure devotion to Christ. (4) For if someone comes and proclaims another Jesus than the one we proclaimed, or if you receive a different spirit from the one you received, or if you accept a different gospel from the one you accepted, you put up with it readily enough.*

Demonic voices speak to our thoughts, reasoning to us the doctrines of demons. Many will not know that they are operating in the doctrine of demons because they will be blinded to truth while walking in deception. ***The worst thing about deception is that those deceived don't know they are in deception.*** One of the attacks against true biblical doctrine among believers is the portrayal that all theology is evil and divisive. The Bible, however, speaks about the traditions of men, beliefs of demons, and the doctrines of God.

We find God's voice in God's doctrine. As believers, we need to embrace the principles or tenets of God and watch out and warn others about the traditions of man and the beliefs of demons. The main message and activity of demonic voices are to accuse, condemn, and cast doubt about the Word of God, the love of God, and the plans of God.

Our heavenly Father is not ashamed or threatened about what He believes and what He declares as truth. Neither should we be so. The voice of the enemy will make us think and confess all doctrine as evil, especially the principles and precepts of God.

> *1 Timothy 4:1 ESV Now the Spirit expressly says that in later times some will depart from the faith by devoting themselves to deceitful spirits and teachings of demons,*
>
> *Revelation 9:20 ESV The rest of mankind, who were not killed by these plagues, did not repent of the works of their hands nor give up worshiping demons and idols of gold and silver and bronze and stone and wood, which cannot see or hear or walk,*

The voices from the demons come to accuse in five different ways.

1. ***The demons accuse us of God.*** They come to us with the accusation that God does not care and does not love us.
2. ***The demons accuse God of us.*** They go before God and accuse us of not loving Him.
3. ***The demons accuse us of others.*** They go to others and speak lies in their ears, which are accusations against us.
4. ***The demons accuse others to us.*** They tell us bad things, lies, and allegations against others so that we would judge them and criticize them.

5. ***The demons accuse us of ourselves.*** The demons tell us that we are wrong, dumb, not forgiven, and that we will never amount to anything. The opposite is also used by the enemy when we listen to his voice. The enemy can accuse us that we are great and beautiful, and God is lucky to have us as one of His children. This type of accusation causes us to be proud and puffed up. God resists the proud and gives grace to the humble. When we believe the charges against ourselves, we walk in rejection and see ourselves as a victim, or we walk in rebellion and pride, therefore limiting the work of God in our lives.

   James 4:6-7 ESV But he gives more grace. Therefore it says, "God opposes the proud but gives grace to the humble." (7) Submit yourselves therefore to God. Resist the devil, and he will flee from you.

What is the essential thing within us that Satan and the demons want? We blame the enemy for affecting our finances, health, or relationships, but the one thing that we have which the enemy intends to rob from our lives is our faith. The only way to please our heavenly Father is a life of faith. Therefore, the enemy seeks to steal that which brings pleasure to God. Consequently, if we listen to the enemy, we will find ourselves in a place of spiritual, emotional, mental, and relational warfare against the will of our heavenly Father. The opposite of being in the Spirit and walking in faith is living and walking in the flesh. We cannot please the Father by walking in the flesh.

> ***Hebrews 11:6 ESV And without faith it is impossible to please him, for whoever would draw near to God must believe that he exists and that he rewards those***

who seek him.

Romans 8:7-8 ESV For the mind that is set on the flesh is hostile to God, for it does not submit to God's law; indeed, it cannot. (8) Those who are in the flesh cannot please God.

Galatians 5:16-17 ESV But I say, walk by the Spirit, and you will not gratify the desires of the flesh. (17) For the desires of the flesh are against the Spirit, and the desires of the Spirit are against the flesh, for these are opposed to each other, to keep you from doing the things you want to do.

THE VOICE OF GOD:

We have looked at the dangers of listening to *our voice*, the *world's voice*, the *voice of the lost religious leaders*, and the *voice of the enemy*. All of these voices compete against us to keep us from hearing **God's voice**. Now that we have covered the four negative voices, let's look at the only sound that matters in life. The fifth voice we hear is that of *our heavenly Father*. The voice of God seems most challenging to listen to and understand because the other sounds are screaming for our attention.

It is certainly easier to grow accustomed to the many distracting voices around us. We need to train our ears to hear the sound of the Father's voice.

KEY THOUGHT:

It is a fantastic reality that the Lord God of the entire universe, all-powerful, all-knowing, and all-present, is waiting to converse with each one of us.

PREPARING OURSELVES TO HEAR GOD'S VOICE

In our world filled with noise, it becomes imperative that we take time each day to be still and listen to the sweet voice of our Father. He might use His Word, angels, His audible voice, preachers, prophets, or any other methods of delivery to get His word and plans to us. The bottom line should be us seeking a daily word from the Creator of the universe personally directed toward us.

John 10:2-4 ESV But he who enters by the door is the shepherd of the sheep. (3) To him the gatekeeper opens. The sheep hear his voice, and he calls his own sheep by name and leads them out. (4) When he has brought out all his own, he goes before them, and the sheep follow him, for they know his voice.

John 10:27 ESV My sheep hear my voice, and I know them, and they follow me.

John 12:28-30 ESV Father, glorify your name." Then a voice came from heaven: "I have glorified it, and I will glorify it again." (29) The crowd that stood there and heard it said that it had thundered. Others said, "An angel has spoken to him." (30) Jesus answered, "This voice has come for your sake, not mine.

Acts 9:3-6 ESV Now as he went on his way, he approached Damascus, and suddenly a light from heaven shone around him. (4) And falling to the ground he heard a voice saying to him, "Saul, Saul, why are you persecuting me?" (5) And he said, "Who are you, Lord?" And he said, "I am Jesus, whom you are persecuting. (6) But rise and enter the city, and you will be told what you are to do."

1 Timothy 4:4-6 ESV For everything created by God is good, and nothing is to be rejected if it is received with thanksgiving, (5) for it is made holy by the word of God and prayer. (6) If you put these things before the brothers, you will be a good servant of Christ Jesus, being trained in the words of the faith and of the good doctrine that you have followed.

1 Timothy 4:13-16 ESV Until I come, devote yourself to the public reading of Scripture, to exhortation, to teaching. (14) Do not neglect the gift you have, which was given you by prophecy when the council of elders laid their hands on you. (15) Practice these things, immerse yourself in them, so that all may see your progress. (16) Keep a close watch on yourself and on the teaching. Persist in this, for by so doing you will save both yourself and your hearers.

1 John 4:6 ESV We are from God. Whoever knows God listens to us; whoever is not from God does not listen to us. By this we know the Spirit of truth and the spirit of error.

Psalms 46:10 KJV Be still, and know that I am God: I will be exalted among the heathen, I will be exalted in the earth.

3

DESIRING TO HEAR GOD'S VOICE

NO WORDS HEARD

Nothing should be more alarming for believers than not getting a Word from the Lord. Think about it. How will we ever know what God truly desires for our lives if we cannot hear from Him? Major decisions like marriage, having children, the buying of a home, relocating to a new city or state, or deciding to transition to a new vocation should not be left up to our emotions, our intellectual reasoning capacities, or happenstance. We should be hearing God's wisdom and leadership in these areas. If we are not faithful in hearing the small daily things of life, how will we hear God in the significant decisions of life?

HEARING, BUT NOT OBEYING

On the other hand, some believers do hear from the Father and receive answers, but the answer they wanted or not in the ways they might have expected, therefore they have a problem with obedience. God's word certainly may come to us in a way that will not fit our paradigm or religious denominational creed. We will not be justified in rejecting that word on the grounds of our religious bias.

It is spiritually dangerous to get a clear word from God about a situation and choose to disobey because of already being emotionally or mentally bound to a personal decision. I did this once in the purchase of a new vehicle and a new house. I knew the Lord did not want me to get either one. Many years ago, I wanted a particular car, and I made it happen through a bank loan. I lost the vehicle through repossession two years later.

Years later, I wanted this new home. I knew I could afford it and had the down payment. I prayed about it, but I was not open to hearing God's voice because no matter what He said, I had already made up my mind. No matter what God had said, I would have listened to what I wanted to hear. Three years later, the housing market crashed, and I was upside down on the house. I knew if I stayed in the home that eventually, the market would come back up, and the value of my home would increase, so I was not worried. However, God woke me up in the middle of the night and told me to move to a new state. The word to relocate was one of clarity; therefore, I couldn't ignore it. The house would not sell, and I had to lose it back to the mortgage lender. In both buying situations, my credit rating hit bottom, and I had to spend years rebuilding what it only took days to ruin.

OUR MENTAL, EMOTIONAL, AND SPIRITUAL PARAMETERS:

When we don't hear God's voice, we can become uncertain of what to do next when faced with good and bad choices. Many times, the wrong life choices don't look so bad or so crazy when we are in the flesh and not listening to the Father's voice. For years now the most common prayer request I have had from believers is their desire to hear the voice of God and to know God's will for their lives. The most commonly asked question I have listened to over the years of ministry is, "How do I hear God's voice?"

Most of the time, the problem of not hearing God is the mental, emotional, and spiritual parameters in which we limit God. By limiting the ways God moves, we limit the ways He might use to speak to us.

We must be willing to change the way we think about how to hear from the Father. In my second book of the "So, You Want To Hear The Voice Of God" series, I list the 15 ways to hear from God and go into detail with each one. In my pastoral experience, I know there are Christian brothers and sisters and Christian leaders who would reject many of the ways I listed in how to hear God's voice. The main reason for this rejection is because it doesn't fit their theological viewpoint.

If we are open to hearing God only one way, and He wants to use a different approach to communicate, we are limiting our ability to hear from Him. We need to stop trying to define "HOW" He will speak to us and just tune our ears to "WHAT" He is saying. It is hard for me to wrap my mind around the fact some believers would refuse a word from the Lord because it didn't come in a way that fits their doctrine. We need to walk in the faith that says, "I don't know how I'm going to hear God today, but His Word says that He speaks to me." We need to believe that He is speaking a message to us and that we will listen with the heart to hear. It is incredible how He reveals Himself to us when we exercise our faith.

Being a Child of God gives us the right to hear His voice. When we don't hear from Him, it is not because He refuses to speak, it is because our heart is not sensitive and tuned to His voice. We know from 1 Peter 2:9 that we can and should hear from the Father.

1 Peter 2:9 ESV But you are a chosen race, a royal

priesthood, a holy nation, a people for his own possession, that you may proclaim the excellencies of him who called you out of darkness into his marvelous light.

The questions are, "How can we respond to God's call if we have not heard?" and "How can we proclaim a message we have not heard?" Our hearing from God will be verified by our proclaiming Him and His wonders.

Some believers deny any means through which God might speak to us except through His written Word. Believing that we can only hear God from the Bible is an extreme viewpoint, which causes many to miss opportunities to listen to what God has in store for them. Remember that our early church fathers had no Bible and operated in faith towards God through oral tradition. They spoke the truths of God, which they had personally received by verbal communication. If we only hear from God through the written Word, then we should shut down Sunday School and Church Services and tell people to stay home and read their Bibles.

IS IT REALLY GOD SPEAKING?

On the flip side of the coin, some believe God speaks in and through everything. These folks may see a number on a clock, a word on a can of food, or the dollar amount from their grocery bill and instantly try to find some spiritual meaning behind it. The positive side is that they are always mindful that the Father can speak to them any time or place, and in a multitude of ways.

The danger of this is being distracted or deceived by what is not God's voice. We risk the threat of being fooled into receiving a perceived Word from God, which the Father didn't give. The Father desires to speak openly and freely to His children. We certainly don't need to try to make that happen through false means and methods. According to Scriptures, hearing God's voice should be a common everyday occurrence among believers. Once we start hearing the Father's sound like a regular activity, we should find ourselves running away from the voices of the strangers.

> *John 10:4-6 ESV When he has brought out all his own, he goes before them, and the sheep follow him, for they know his voice. (5) A stranger they will not follow, but they will flee from him, for they do not know the voice of strangers." (6) This figure of speech Jesus used with them, but they did not understand what he was saying to them.*
>
> *John 10:27 ESV My sheep hear my voice, and I know them, and they follow me.*

YOU CANNOT TEACH AND GIVE WHAT YOU DO NOT POSSESS

The priest Eli was supposed to be accustomed to hearing the voice of God. After all, he was the priest. If anyone could listen to and recognize God's voice, one would think that it should have been Eli, the priest. However, at some point during his ministry in the temple, Eli grew accustomed to the rituals of his position. This familiarity resulted in Eli moving away from the essential things. He got so focused on religious activities that represent God, that he missed God. This everyday routine kept him around the "things" of God, yet he was missing the reality of God's voice and God's presence.

Hannah, on the other hand, was a God-fearing woman who had prayed for years for a child. She had an ongoing relationship with God, whereby open conversation was normal. The Lord gave her a son, and she named him Samuel. Hannah brought Samuel for nurturing in the ways of the Lord to Eli the Priest in the temple.

One night, God spoke to Samuel by calling out his name. The young lad didn't recognize the heavenly voice. Some would say that it was because of his young age and inexperience, which would surely factor into the equation. However, the main reason the young lad did not recognize the voice of the heavenly Father speaking was that Eli the Priest had not trained him in this area of hearing God's voice. One cannot give what one does not possess.

When the lad went to Eli to see what he wanted, Eli didn't realize what Samuel was experiencing. Eli's first reaction offered no help to Samuel because hearing God's voice had become something Eli no longer personally recognized himself. The ministry of hearing God's voice had become a lost art somewhere in Eli's past. Imagine sitting under a pastor who no longer hears the sound of the Father in some form and manner. Imagine a Pastor needing to get his sermons out of another man's material because the pastor no longer received illumination from God.

After three encounters, Eli realized that God was summoning Samuel. Imagine, God was speaking to the young lad. Samuel grew up to be a mighty Prophet of God, who heard and spoke the deep secrets of God and the throne room out to the nations and the kings. It was that time in the temple as a young lad encountering the voice of God that molded him to have ears to hear the Father's voice. This story should be a guide to us in realizing that no matter what our position, we may have times where we do not recognize the voice of the Father. We need to be still and say, "Speak Lord, your servant is listening."

> *1 Samuel 3:3-11 ESV The lamp of God had not yet gone out, and Samuel was lying down in the temple of the LORD, where the ark of God was. (4) Then the LORD called Samuel, and he said, "Here I am!" (5) and ran to Eli and said, "Here I am, for you called me." But he said, "I did not call; lie down again." So he went and lay down. (6) And the LORD called again, "Samuel!" and Samuel arose and went to Eli and said, "Here I am, for you called me." But he said, "I did not call, my son; lie down again." (7) Now Samuel did not yet know the LORD, and the word of the LORD had not yet been revealed to him. (8) And the LORD called Samuel again the third time. And he arose and went to Eli and said, "Here I am, for you called me." Then Eli perceived that the LORD was calling the boy. (9) Therefore Eli said to Samuel, "Go, lie down, and if he calls you, you shall say, 'Speak, LORD, for your servant hears.'" So Samuel went and lay down in his place. (10) And the LORD came and stood, calling as at other times, "Samuel! Samuel!" And Samuel said, "Speak, for your servant hears." (11)   Then the LORD said to Samuel, "Behold, I am about to do a thing in Israel at which the two ears of everyone who hears it will tingle.*

THE VOICES OF THOSE WHOM WE LOVE

Think of a newborn baby placed in the arms of his mother for the first time. He seems to recognize his mom's voice already because he has heard it as she carried him before birth. The mother's voice is familiar. Soon the same will be right with the sound of the father. After just a short time, the mother or father can enter the room and say something, and the young baby will respond with a smile, or the jerk of his hands and feet because he recognizes their voices.

When we hear the voice of our mothers, our wives, or our children, we know immediately who these loved ones are. When they call on the phone, they don't need to identify themselves because when they start to speak, we instantly recognize who it is. Why is that? Over time we learn to know and determine the voice of our loved ones. Suppose close family members were walking down the road and were a far distance away, we could still tell they were our family members. We would be able to identify them because of their distinct walk, hand motions, body language, or how they carried themselves.

THE SHEEP LEARNING OF THE SHEPHERD

When our Lord Jesus Christ said that His sheep would know His voice and follow Him, He was not speaking about some magical spell He placed on people once they became Christians. It was not some supernatural impartation that we would automatically know His voice.

How do the sheep get to know the voice of the Shepherd? It comes from the relationship of getting to know the Shepherd. In this experience of knowing the Shepherd, there comes a trust knowing the Shepherd will always work what is best for the sheep. We learn the voice of the Shepherd, our Lord Jesus Christ, and our Heavenly Father, through an ongoing relationship and fellowship. The more we fellowship with the Father, the more we are in tune with His voice and recognize how and when He speaks.

THE RELIGIOUS THINGS OF GOD CAN BE A DISTRACTION FROM HEARING GOD

We should realize that we do not learn to hear the Father's voice when we are being bombarded with noise, even if it is "Christian music." We need to be intentional in making time to tune out other voices and sounds to be able to hear the Father's voice. Tuning out so we can tune in includes the things that we would classify as "Christian." When our Lord wanted to hear from the Father, He went to the mountains alone, even separating Himself from the synagogue and His disciples. We might think that the church building would be the most natural place to hear the Father's voice. However, the things that represent God and the Christian walk can get in the way of fellowshipping with God. Church life can be so active and busy that sometimes we need to escape to "our mountain place" to commune with the Father.

4

WE ARE CREATED FOR GOD'S PLEASURE

Think for a minute on these questions. Why were we created, and are we here on this earth? What is the meaning of our existence, and what are we to do with our lives? There certainly must be more to life than getting a job and making a living until we retire and die.

We read in Scriptures that God created humanity to give the heavenly Father pleasure. It is paramount that we hear the Father's voice so that we can be children of faith and sons and daughters who honor and please the Father. We don't need to belittle ourselves by thinking that we are "nobodies" and unworthy of hearing the voice of God. God is not a respecter of persons. In the Word of God, we find people from all walks of life conversing with the Father. We see the highly educated to those with little or no education, and those who range economically from rags to riches. Within the Scriptures, we see ordinary people, kings, priests, and prophets who turned their ear to the voice of the Creator of the universe. When it comes to being able to hear God's voice, the Father is not a respecter of persons.

> *Revelation 4:11 ESV "Worthy are you, our Lord and God, to receive glory and honor and power, for you created all things, and by your will they existed and were created."*

> *Hebrews 11:6 ESV And without faith it is impossible to please him, for whoever would draw near to God must believe that he exists and that he rewards those who seek him.*

> *1 Corinthians 1:26-28 ESV (26) For consider your calling, brothers: not many of you were wise according to worldly standards, not many were powerful, not many were of noble birth. (27) But God chose what is foolish in the world to shame the wise; God chose what is weak in the world to shame the strong; (28) God chose what is low and despised in the world, even things that are not, to bring to nothing things that are,*

THE FATHER DELIGHTS OVER US

God delights in revealing Himself to His children. He loves to speak to us, although we may, at times, be surprised in His ways of communication. God is filled with "suddenlies" as our heavenly Father moves upon His body with His presence. There is certainly no limitation to God or the way He moves or works. Communicating with the Father includes many different methods that the Godhead uses to speak to His children. Our God is so great and marvelous, He certainly will not limit Himself to the ways He imparts His wisdom, will, and ways to His children.

> *Jeremiah 33:2-3 ESV "Thus says the LORD who made the earth, the LORD who formed it to establish it—the LORD is his name: (3) Call to me and I will answer you, and will tell you great and hidden things that you have not known.*

In this book, we will mainly discuss methods to follow to hear God's voice. In book 2 of the series, entitled "The 15 Ways To Hear God's Voice," I discuss in detail the many different ways the Father speaks to us. In no way can any book contain all the means and methods the Father uses to communicate to His children. Some of how the Father speaks to His children are accepted and expected by many. However, the Father also uses those unexpected forms of communication, which we need to explore and embrace, so we don't miss an opportunity of communion and fellowship. Remember, God created us for His pleasure.

The purpose of this book is for us to learn to tune and turn our ears towards God and hear the message He has for us. We will see that although hearing God's voice is a supernatural experience, it should also be a regular daily activity for the believer. This book, however, is not intended to create a formula of "do these steps" to hear God. We desire to see Christian believers cultivate a deep personal relationship and fellowship with the Father that is grounded and based on His Word, faith, and trust. We desire to see believers hear and receive what the Father has for them.

> *Job 33:14-16 ESV For God speaks in one way, and in two, though man does not perceive it. (15) In a dream, in a vision of the night, when deep sleep falls on men, while they slumber on their beds, (16) then he opens the ears of men and terrifies them with warnings,*

THOSE WHO HEARD GOD'S VOICE WERE HISTORY MAKERS

It is an incredible privilege to be able to speak directly to God, our Father, the creator of the universe, and have

Him speak back to us as His children. One of the truths that we need to embrace as a healthy activity is that *God created us to commune with Him*. That is why we have the opening chapters of Genesis showing God and Adam walking together in the Garden of Eden. The last chapters of the Bible picture us back walking with the Father in the New City on the New Earth. The Bible starts with and ends with humanity having deep personal communion with the Father. Everything else between the first and last chapters is about teaching men about God's redemptive nature to restore humankind to proper relationship and fellowship.

The Lord is ready, willing, and able to speak to us. We must know how to listen with the heart of obedience, and most importantly, we must know how to be sure it is the Father speaking. Sometimes God will intervene in an unexpected way, which may seem to us to be the voice of the enemy. In the Word of God, we find over and over the Father speaking, and man is hearing and obeying. The results are changed lives and the writing of redemptive history.

For a moment, could we possibility imagine ourselves in the shoes (or sandals) of a Bible character? Could we, for a moment, see ourselves placed in Balaam's shoes as he listened to his donkey rebuking him as the Word of God came from the mouth of an animal? This story brings us to an important point. Not all that God speaks will be "feel-good" blessings. Many times, the words from the Father are words of instruction, correction, rebuke, or guidance.

> *Numbers 22:27-28 ESV When the donkey saw the angel of the LORD, she lay down under Balaam. And Balaam's anger was kindled, and he struck the donkey with his staff. (28) Then the LORD opened*

the mouth of the donkey, and she said to Balaam, "What have I done to you, that you have struck me these three times?"

Could we see ourselves in Moses' shoes as he listened to the voice of God coming from a burning bush? God was calling Moses to be the one to deliver the Israelites out of the hands of Pharaoh and Egypt. Drastic times require drastic measures. God does not waste His time speaking words of the deliverance of a people and the breaking down strongholds when there is no one to hear and stand in the gap. Will God speak over your city to Christians who have not learned to listen to God in the smallest areas of possessing their soul and body as vessels of honor. He only gives great things to those who have learned to be faithful in little things.

> *Exodus 3:2-6 ESV   And the angel of the LORD appeared to him in a flame of fire out of the midst of a bush. He looked, and behold, the bush was burning, yet it was not consumed. (3) And Moses said, "I will turn aside to see this great sight, why the bush is not burned." (4) When the LORD saw that he turned aside to see, God called to him out of the bush, "Moses, Moses!" And he said, "Here I am." (5) Then he said, "Do not come near; take your sandals off your feet, for the place on which you are standing is holy ground." (6) And he said, "I am the God of your father, the God of Abraham, the God of Isaac, and the God of Jacob." And Moses hid his face, for he was afraid to look at God.*

Again, could we or would we want to be placed in Adam's position (no shoes, or other items of clothing), in the

Garden of Eden as he and Eve experienced walking and talking with God each day?

> *Genesis 3:8 ESV And they heard the sound of the LORD God walking in the garden in the cool of the day, and the man and his wife hid themselves from the presence of the LORD God among the trees of the garden.*

Moses had been the leader of the wilderness group for forty years, and then he died. There was a passing of the mantle on to Joshua, who had walked with Moses the full forty years. Could you place yourself in Joshua's shoes as he listened to God's voice commanding him to cross over the Jordan and possess the land? The time of wilderness wandering is at an end, and it is now time to fight and possess the land.

> *Joshua 1:1-3 ESV After the death of Moses the servant of the LORD, the LORD said to Joshua the son of Nun, Moses' assistant, (2) "Moses my servant is dead. Now therefore arise, go over this Jordan, you and all this people, into the land that I am giving to them, to the people of Israel. (3) Every place that the sole of your foot will tread upon I have given to you, just as I promised to Moses.*

> *Joshua 1:5-7 ESV No man shall be able to stand before you all the days of your life. Just as I was with Moses, so I will be with you. I will not leave you or forsake you. (6) Be strong and courageous, for you shall cause this people to inherit the land that I swore to their fathers to give them. (7) Only be strong and very courageous, being careful to do*

according to all the law that Moses my servant commanded you. Do not turn from it to the right hand or to the left, that you may have good success wherever you go.

What if Joshua had not trained under the leadership of Moses? What if he had not learned the art of listening, hearing, and obeying the voice of God? How could Joshua possibly know God's strategy for taking more than two million people across the Jordan River and possessing the land of promise? Had he not heard from God he would have tried conventional military warfare in attacking Jericho instead of God's strategy of circling the city in faith. What if he purposed in his heart not to hear or obey the voice of God?

Joshua 1:16-17 ESV And they answered Joshua, "All that you have commanded us we will do, and wherever you send us we will go. (17) Just as we obeyed Moses in all things, so we will obey you. Only may the LORD your God be with you, as he was with Moses!

THOSE WHO WOULD NOT HEAR GOD'S VOICE:

Once the Israelites reached the Promised Land, the people stopped listening to God. It is one thing to be deaf to the voice of the Father, but it is something entirely different to become dull of hearing and then outright disobey. Eight times Moses came down the mountain with commands from the Lord God Almighty. The first six times, the people listened to what Moses said and repeated together, "All that the Lord has spoken we will do." On the seventh trip down the mountain, Moses found the people having an orgy around a golden calf.

In the KJV of the Bible, Proverbs 29:18 talks about vision. It says that if we do not have a vision, we will perish. In studying this verse, I found that the KJV does not do translation justice. The better or more accurate translation of the Hebrew is in the ESV.

> *Proverbs 29:18 ESV Where there is no prophetic vision the people cast off restraint, but blessed is he who keeps the law.*

The meaning behind Proverbs 29:18 is that if we don't have spiritual guidance by hearing the voice of God, the people will cast off God's law and order and do what is right in their own eyes. When spiritual guidance left our school system, they had to replace it with police officers in the halls to try to maintain some form of law and order.

It is essential that we "hearken" to the voice of the Father. To "hearken" means to hear with the full intent to obey. One of the reasons some believers today do not understand God's voice is because they refused to obey a previous command from the Lord, or they naturally walk in the heart of rebellion. Ouch! *If we are not faithful in a little, we will not receive more.*

> *2 Chronicles 33:9-11 ESV (9) Manasseh led Judah and the inhabitants of Jerusalem astray, to do more evil than the nations whom the LORD destroyed before the people of Israel. (10) The LORD spoke to Manasseh and to his people, but they paid no attention. (11) Therefore the LORD brought upon them the commanders of the army of the king of Assyria, who captured Manasseh with hooks and bound him with chains of bronze and brought him to*

Babylon.

2 Chronicles 36:15-16 ESV (15) The LORD, the God of their fathers, sent persistently to them by his messengers, because he had compassion on his people and on his dwelling place. (16) But they kept mocking the messengers of God, despising his words and scoffing at his prophets, until the wrath of the LORD rose against his people, until there was no remedy.

Nehemiah 9:29-30 ESV And you warned them in order to turn them back to your law. Yet they acted presumptuously and did not obey your commandments, but sinned against your rules, which if a person does them, he shall live by them, and they turned a stubborn shoulder and stiffened their neck and would not obey. (30) Many years you bore with them and warned them by your Spirit through your prophets. Yet they would not give ear. Therefore you gave them into the hand of the peoples of the lands.

Jeremiah 25:4-7 ESV You have neither listened nor inclined your ears to hear, although the LORD persistently sent to you all his servants the prophets, (5) saying, 'Turn now, every one of you, from his evil way and evil deeds, and dwell upon the land that the LORD has given to you and your fathers from of old and forever. (6) Do not go after other gods to serve and worship them, or provoke me to anger with the work of your hands. Then I will do you no harm.' (7) Yet you have not listened to me, declares the LORD, that you might provoke me to anger with the work of your hands to your own harm.

Matthew 13:14-15 ESV   Indeed, in their case the prophecy of Isaiah is fulfilled that says: "'"You will indeed hear but never understand, and you will indeed see but never perceive." (15) For this people's heart has grown dull, and with their ears they can barely hear, and their eyes they have closed, lest they should see with their eyes and hear with their ears and understand with their heart and turn, and I would heal them.'

Some believers live and operate typically as crisis-oriented people. They don't think about the art of hearing God's voice daily when things are going well but are quick to want a Word from God when a crisis finds their address and comes to their lives. When it looks like they will lose their family, their job, their home, or their health, they are quick to desire prayer for a quick "fix-all" word from God. In the crisis, they are ready to dial God's 911 number for help in trouble. God's 911 number could be Psalms 50:15.

Psalms 50:15 ESV   and call upon me in the day of trouble; I will deliver you, and you shall glorify me."

Don't get me wrong; the Father cares for us and wants us to turn to Him in our 911 crisis moments. However, He also wants us to turn to Him in our good times with the same passion and intense drive as when we are in our crisis mode. It is the heart of the Father that we hear and communicate with Him all the time, especially when things seem to be going well.

Could you imagine walking in your front door each day after work, and your child runs up to you and asks, "What did you bring me?" The heart of a father or mother longs for their children to run to their arms each day for no other reason than a love relationship. They want their children desiring nothing else except the sweet fellowship of their parents. Like any earthly father, our heavenly Father doesn't want to see our communication with Him limited to "need-based" crisis communication. This type of prayer will still touch the heart of the Father because He is gracious and merciful, but there is so much more to communicate with and from the Father then a "help me" encounter. He desires to have sweet fellowship time with us as we hear His voice and respond with praise and adoration.

Again, I must say that God created us for His pleasure. I happen to believe that if God can speak through a donkey and a burning bush, He certainly can and will talk to and through us. I think that by the end of this book, if the readers desire to hear from the Lord, they will do so. Even before reading the second book on the 15 ways to hear God's voice, the reader will experience newfound joy in communicating with the Father. For those of us who already understand from the Lord, maybe we will find new ways for God to speak to and through us.

We have laid some necessary foundations for hearing the voice of the Father. Join us as we walk the journey of preparation in seeking our Lord's face together and discovering the ways of hearing the voice of God.

5

BE READY TO LISTEN – FOR GOD IS SPEAKING

We are continuing with the preparation for hearing God's voice. Have an expectation! We must expect that we are going to get a Word from the Lord every day and in every situation. One of the buzz statements of today is, "God will always meet us at the level of our expectation." We need to have a sense of expectation to hear God's voice. We should be reading this book with our Bible, a journal pad, and a pen readily available. Please read all the Scriptures given in their full context and make notes as the Holy Spirit reveals the truth.

GOD IS ONLINE, ARE WE?

We must remember that it is not an issue of the Father speaking, but a matter of our hearing what He is saying. Before we continue reading, please pray against any spiritual deafness that you may be encountering. The Bible teaches us that before we become deaf to His Word, we slide into a state called "dull of hearing." Ask the Lord to forgive and heal anything that has caused spiritual deafness or dullness of hearing. We should ask the Lord to open our spiritual ears, our mind, and our hearts to hear and to receive His Word today. It is so important that we have ears that are "tuned" to the voice of the Father. We must not allow ourselves to become dull in hearing.

Matthew 13:14-15 ESV   Indeed, in their case the prophecy of Isaiah is fulfilled that says: "'"You will indeed hear but never understand, and you will indeed see but never perceive." (15) For this people's heart has grown dull, and with their ears they can barely hear, and their eyes they have closed, lest they should see with their eyes and hear with their ears and understand with their heart and turn, and I would heal them.'

Hebrews 5:11 ESV   About this we have much to say, and it is hard to explain, since you have become dull of hearing.

The first thing we need to establish as truth within our hearts is the doctrinal belief that God is speaking today. The second thing we need to develop as truth within our hearts is that we, as believers, can hear God's voice. Some would say that God has given us His written Word, the Bible, what else do we need? They would say there is no need for any other means of hearing God's voice. It is true that the Bible is the inerrant Word of God and is the primary means by which the Father speaks to us today. The Bible is the ultimate authority in all matters and the standard whereby we judge all other means of communication, for God cannot contradict His Word or His character.

Question. Why would we pray if we do not believe that God answers? If God answers prayer, how would we know that answer if there were no other means to hear God's voice other than the Bible? Example. I am praying about buying a house. There is not one Scripture I can go to that will say do or do not purchase that house. Therefore, I need to hear a word from God about what I should do.

There are Scriptures about letting the peace of God rule our hearts. But what if I don't know those Scriptures, nor do I know how to walk in or recognize God's peace? Therefore, we need every possible way that God has established to communicate with Him.

To be fair now about the overuse of the term, "God told me." On the flip side, some preface every statement they make with "God told me." It may not be precisely that statement, for I've heard "The Lord was telling me," "God spoke to me," or "I received a word from God," used by folks to preface each statement they make in a conversation. This "God told me," opening statement makes it difficult to disagree with because it leaves everyone who is listening feel as if they would be arguing with God if they disagreed.

This overuse of "God said" is abuse by those who feel they need a voice over others and their opinions strengthened, validated, and accepted. Is God speaking to these people about every statement, or are these folks who claim to "hear from God" about everything just bonkers? Don't throw the baby out with the wash. Of course, we will always have extremes. Of course, there will be those who want to give God credit (or blame) for every statement they make. However, on the other side, some don't believe God speaks at all outside of His Word, the Bible. The key is a balanced Biblical approach. It would help us to read the "sheep hear my voice" Scriptures once again.

> *John 10:3-4 ESV To him the gatekeeper opens. The sheep hear his voice, and he calls his own sheep by name and leads them out. (4) When he has brought out all his own, he goes before them, and the sheep follow him, for they know his voice.*
>
> *John 10:16 ESV And I have other sheep that are not of*

this fold. I must bring them also, and they will listen to my voice. So there will be one flock, one shepherd.

John 10:26-27 ESV but you do not believe because you are not among my sheep. (27) My sheep hear my voice, and I know them, and they follow me.

There are many questions concerning God speaking to us in our day.
- Is God speaking to us today?
- If God is speaking to us today, how is He doing it?
- If God is speaking to us today, what is He saying?
- If God is speaking to us today, will He speak to me?
- If God is speaking to us today, how can I discern His voice from all the other voices?

WRITING HIS WORD ON OUR HEART

Our focus now needs to examine some Old Testament Scriptures concerning hearing the voice of God. The shadow of the Old Testament becomes substance in the New Testament. To establish the teaching from God's Word correctly, we need to build line upon line and precept upon precept. If we are making a doctrinal statement from the substance of the New Testament, we should be able to find an Old Testament shadow.

Jeremiah 31:33 ESV For this is the covenant that I will make with the house of Israel after those days, declares the LORD: I will put my law within them, and I will write it on their hearts. And I will be their God, and they shall be my people.

In Jeremiah 31:33, God spoke through the prophet, declaring that a day was coming in the distant future when He would place His Word in the minds and the hearts of His people. Bless God, that day came. That day took its fulfillment when our Lord Jesus Christ came and walked among men, and the Word became flesh and dwelt among us.

John 1:1-3 ESV In the beginning was the Word, and the Word was with God, and the Word was God. (2) He was in the beginning with God. (3) All things were made through him, and without him was not any thing made that was made.

John 1:14 ESV And the Word became flesh and dwelt among us, and we have seen his glory, glory as of the only Son from the Father, full of grace and truth.

It was at this point that men moved by the Holy Spirit begin to write down the words that our Lord Jesus Christ said and the works that He did. Everything about the life of our Lord is an exact representation of God talking to us. The Word became flesh and dwelt among us.

2 Timothy 3:16 ESV All Scripture is breathed out by God and profitable for teaching, for reproof, for correction, and for training in righteousness,

2 Peter 1:20-21 ESV knowing this first of all, that no prophecy of Scripture comes from someone's own interpretation. (21) For no prophecy was ever produced by the will of man, but men spoke from God as they were carried along by the Holy Spirit.

Continuing with the explanation of Jeremiah 31:33, God said that He would write His Word in the inner parts and on our hearts. Do you remember, in John 20, when our Lord Jesus Christ rose from the dead and appeared to His disciples in a closed room?

John 20:19-22 ESV On the evening of that day, the first day of the week, the doors being locked where the disciples were for fear of the Jews, Jesus came and stood among them and said to them, "Peace be with you." (20) When he had said this, he showed them his hands and his side. Then the disciples were glad when they saw the Lord. (21) Jesus said to them again, "Peace be with you. As the Father has sent me, even so I am sending you." (22) And when he had said this, he breathed on them and said to them, "Receive the Holy Spirit.

The Lord Jesus Christ breathed on them, and they received the indwelling Holy Spirit. This indwelling is the same experience with the Holy Spirit we experienced when we called on the Lord Jesus Christ to become saved. The Person of the Holy Spirit comes within us, and He takes up residence and ownership, and He adopts us and positions us into the family of God. This event in John 20:19-22 is the fulfillment of the Jeremiah 31:33 passage as the Lord put His Word and His life into us in the Person of the Holy Spirit. He began to write His word upon our hearts.

When the Holy Spirit came to dwell within us, all that God is, including His Word and His character, came to reside within us. The Person of the Holy Spirit dwelling within us, with all the character traits and attributes of God, allows us the ability to hear God in our mind and our heart. Because we have the Spirit of God, we can know the mind of God. If we can see the mind of God, then we know that God is speaking.

> *1 Corinthians 2:9-14 ESV (9) But, as it is written, "What no eye has seen, nor ear heard, nor the heart of man imagined, what God has prepared for those who love him"— (10) these things God has revealed to us through the Spirit. For the Spirit searches everything, even the depths of God. (11) For who knows a person's thoughts except the spirit of that person, which is in him? So also no one comprehends the thoughts of God except the Spirit of God. (12) Now we have received not the spirit of the world, but the Spirit who is from God, that we might understand the things freely given us by God. (13) And we impart this in words not taught by human wisdom but taught by the Spirit, interpreting spiritual truths to those who are spiritual. (14) The natural person does not accept the things of the Spirit of God, for they are folly to him, and he is not able to understand them because they are spiritually discerned.*

Because God has given us His Holy Spirit and because His Spirit brings God's Word, will, and ways, we can hear God's voice better than any other time in history. The problem is all the other stuff that comes at us. To listen to God's voice, we need to know how to overcome all the different sounds and push through the thing that gets in the way of us hearing our heavenly Father. We need to distinguish between God talking and our thoughts. We continuously have random thoughts, and we need to discern between our random thoughts and the actual voice of the Father within us.

THE LONGING TO HEAR.

Hearing God's voice is something we, as God's children, should long for, but many of us didn't know that it was so hard to do. God wants us to hear His voice more than we want to listen to it. He doesn't speak to us through liver shivers or goosebumps. However, the excitement and awesomeness of responsibility of hearing God may result in us having liver shivers or goosebumps. The critical point is how we hear God's voice without being "bogged down" with the emotional or physical manifestations that may occur in the process.

Hearing the voice of God should be as natural as hearing our best friend talking to us. What's more, we can listen to Him every day and not just on special occasions. Did you know that it is easier for lost people to hear about and speak about the birth of Christ around Christmas time than any other time of the year? Why? They expect hearing due to the season. Therefore, they are more open to hearing from the Father. What if they had that expectation all year?

It is this way of hearing God's voice. It should be a natural daily all-year-round activity, but it seems we have better ears to hear at special events, conferences, or revivals. The Father speaks to us in the natural moments of life, taking away the mystical dynamics of desiring to hear Him. There will always be those who try to make the hearing of God's voice some weird magical hoodoo voodoo. Ignore those who try to make hearing God a mystical experience. It is, however, a supernatural event when a sinful, weak human has the religious right and blessing to converse with the One Most High God, Creator of the universe. The key is to keep it straightforward and honest. The Father is waiting.

REACH OUT AND TOUCH SOMEONE, (TOUCHING GOD)

We live in a day in which almost everyone has a cell phone. This author can remember back in the late 1980s and early 1990s when visiting Robin Harchak, a fellow pastor who worked as a Christian camp director in Pennsylvania. Robin had a monster-sized bag phone that he carried with him everywhere he went. He kept telling us that it would soon become a routine daily lifestyle for all people to have a portable phone. The response he received revealed our feelings about phones. We told him that it was just a fad, and like every other fad, it would run its course and phase out. Boy, were we wrong, and wow, Robin was right. Now it seems that every family member has a mobile phone.

Many of us have been in restaurants where we watched three people sitting at a table together all on their phones talking to faceless voices. The whole time they seemed uninterested in communicating with those seated in the restaurant next to them. Some of it is nothing more than speaking empty words in endless conversations with superficial friends. We all can relate as to how difficult it is to be still, to be quiet, and listen while surrounded by this fast-paced, noisy society. Can we say the same thing about our fellowship with God? He lives within us and desires communication, but we seem to be busy, busy, busy. I've seen believers gather for prayer meetings at the church, and they spend most of the time conversing with one another. Many times, the topics were unrelated to prayer needs. If pure daily communion with the Father were comfortable for the believer, everyone would do it.

CROWDED SWITCHBOARDS:

Husbands, we may find at times that the voices of the TV come between communication with our wives and us. We may sit together in the living room for hours without speaking to one another. Seated in the same room focused on the TV is certainly not what would be classified as quality time together or qualified as communication. Then when either the husband or wife speaks, the other does not hear because of having our hearing tuned and turned to something else. The reason I said all this is because of the many different voices speaking to us every day, all day long. These voices crowd out the sound of our Heavenly Father, just like we can tune out our spouse or our children.

Suppose I want a tall cold glass of fresh milk; however, I only have one glass, and that glass currently has tomato juice in it. To fill the glass with milk, I must make room. To make room, I need to do something with the tomato juice. The same is valid with God's voice versus all the other voices. When the sounds of the world, the lost religious leaders, the demonic enemy, and my voice has crowed out our hearing, the average Christian has no room for listening when the Father does speak.

Imagine that the many ways our Father speaks to us are like an old telephone switchboard. Suppose God has a switchboard with many different phone numbers. The Lord may be calling, and yet we can be so unaccustomed to His voice that we are not sure who is speaking. An excellent example of this from the Bible is Samuel, the young prophet in training. We talked earlier about Eli the Priest had lost his ear to hear God and therefore was not expecting a message from God to come to the Temple area. But also, in this story, we find a young lad in the school of the prophets learning to speak God's Word, yet he was unaccustomed and untrained in hearing God's Word. How can we express forth what we have not heard?

> *1 Samuel 3:3-10 ESV The lamp of God had not yet gone out, and Samuel was lying down in the temple of the LORD, where the ark of God was. (4) Then the LORD called Samuel, and he said, "Here I am!" (5) and ran to Eli and said, "Here I am, for you called me." But he said, "I did not call; lie down again." So he went and lay down. (6) And the LORD called again, "Samuel!" and Samuel arose and went to Eli and said, "Here I am, for you called me." But he said, "I did not call, my son; lie down again." (7) Now Samuel did not yet know the LORD, and the word of the LORD had not yet been revealed to him. (8) And the LORD called Samuel again the third time. And he arose and went to Eli and said, "Here I am, for you called me." Then Eli perceived that the LORD was calling the boy. (9) Therefore Eli said to Samuel, "Go, lie down, and if he calls you, you shall say, 'Speak, LORD, for your servant hears.'" So Samuel went and lay down in his place. (10) And the LORD came and stood, calling as at other times, "Samuel! Samuel!" And Samuel said, "Speak, for your servant hears."*

We have heard the phrase, "Don't throw the baby out with the bathwater." We all have met someone who said that God told them something, and we knew that it did not line up with the Word of God or the character of God. Therefore, we could not come in agreement with their assessment of what they believed God was saying. Many of us pastors have heard things like, "God told me that woman is to be my wife." The problem was that she was married to someone else and had children. Well, most people would quickly recognize that the statement was not from God, and the person speaking had been captured by lust and was coveting another man's wife.

Some of the hardest discussions I have entered was when I found myself attempting to correct someone who believed they had received a word of the Lord, which did not line up with the Word of God or the character of God. It should be clear to us that not everyone who claims to have a "word from the Lord" is right about the origin of that word. We, as believers, can become so emotionally or mentality tied to something or someone that we convince ourselves we have received a word from God about it.

The Father has warned us in His word concerning those who claimed to have a "word from God," and yet God had not spoken to them. Just because we have seen abuses with those who pretend to have received a word from the Lord, does not mean that God doesn't speak.

> *Jeremiah 23:16-18 ESV Thus says the LORD of hosts: "Do not listen to the words of the prophets who prophesy to you, filling you with vain hopes. They speak visions of their own minds, not from the mouth of the LORD. (17) They say continually to those who despise the word of the LORD, 'It shall be well with you'; and to everyone who stubbornly follows his own heart, they say, 'No disaster shall come upon you.'" (18) For who among them has stood in the council of the LORD to see and to hear his word, or who has paid attention to his word and listened?*

> *Jeremiah 23:21-26 ESV "I did not send the prophets, yet they ran; I did not speak to them, yet they prophesied. (22) But if they had stood in my council, then they would have proclaimed my words to my people, and they would have turned them from their evil way, and from the evil of their deeds. (23) "Am I a God at hand, declares the LORD, and not a God far away? (24) Can a man hide himself in secret places so that I cannot see him? declares the LORD. Do I not fill heaven and earth? declares the LORD. (25) I have heard what the prophets have said who prophesy lies in my name, saying, 'I have dreamed, I have dreamed!' (26) How long shall there be lies in the heart of the prophets who prophesy lies, and who prophesy the deceit of their own heart,*

We should still endeavor to seek God's voice daily in our lives. There are two statements I use when dealing with people and their lack of understanding in hearing God's voice. Remember this statement I have already given. "Don't throw the baby out with the bathwater." We should not abandon the daily experiences of hearing God speak just because others may abuse it. The other statement is, "Chew up the fat and spit out the bones." Having spiritual discernment will help us keep in perspective that there may be some truth in what people are saying and not to disregard everything based on the error. This discernment comes from handling the Word of God correctly.

> *Hebrews 5:11-14 ESV About this we have much to say, and it is hard to explain, since you have become dull of hearing. (12) For though by this time you ought to be teachers, you need someone to teach you again the basic principles of the oracles of God. You*

need milk, not solid food, (13) for everyone who lives on milk is unskilled in the word of righteousness, since he is a child. (14) But solid food is for the mature, for those who have their powers of discernment trained by constant practice to distinguish good from evil.

6

WHY DO WE WANT TO HEAR FROM GOD?

Why should we want to hear God's voice? That may sound like a silly question, but motives are important in anything we do, especially in spiritual and kingdom matters. We have encountered people seeking a word from the Lord with improper motives. Many forms of manipulation are present within the body of Christ. There have been some who spoke the "word of God" who used this activity as a form of manipulation. People looking to hear something from God can be most vulnerable to manipulation from those who driven to speak something. This manipulation can come from those seeking, receiving, and giving the word. Asking the Father and hearing His voice is a spiritual discipline that carries a high reward and a great responsibility. We are not supposed to seek Him passively; we are to seek Him diligently.

> *Hebrews 11:6 ESV And without faith it is impossible to please him, for whoever would draw near to God must believe that he exists and that he rewards those who seek him.*
>
> *Matthew 6:33 ESV But seek first the kingdom of God and his righteousness, and all these things will be added to you.*

> *Psalms 105:3-4 ESV Glory in his holy name; let the hearts of those who seek the LORD rejoice! (4) Seek the LORD and his strength; seek his presence continually!*

> *Proverbs 8:17 ESV I love those who love me, and those who seek me diligently find me.*

Our Lord commanded us many times in Scriptures to hear and understand. If we do not listen and understand, we will honor the Lord with our lips, but our hearts will be far from Him. If we do not hear and understand God's word, we will worship in vain and elevate the traditions and doctrines of man over the Word of God.

> *Proverbs 4:7 ESV The beginning of wisdom is this: Get wisdom, and whatever you get, get insight.*

> *Matthew 15:8-10 ESV "'This people honors me with their lips, but their heart is far from me; (9) in vain do they worship me, teaching as doctrines the commandments of men.'" (10) And he called the people to him and said to them, "Hear and understand:*

> *John 8:43 ESV Why do you not understand what I say? It is because you cannot bear to hear my word.*

PROPER MOTIVATION FOR DESIRING TO HEAR GOD'S VOICE:

Many of us have seen some who used the prophetic voice to manipulate people or to share something on their heart they feared to share in their conversation. We can witness this a lot in prayer meetings. People are supposed to be hearing from God and then speaking back to the Father what they hear. However, some prayer meetings become notorious for people expressing things in "prayer" to one another in the name of God that they fear to say outside of that setting. It is like they are seeking to have their statements of gossip validated by saying it is a word from God.

A man in a particular church in Pennsylvania had a "Word from the Lord" to share in every church service. Years before he came to our church, another church group had hurt this man relationally and emotionally and he carried a heart of unforgiveness, hurt and anger. Every time he gave a "prophetic word from the Lord," it conveyed his hurt and anger, and which filled his "word from the Lord" with condemnation and judgment. It was not that the prophetic word was completely wrong because he received specific things from the Lord. He had learned to tune his ears to hear what the Spirit was saying to the church. However, the heart-baggage which the word had to go through made it condemning and judgmental when it exited his mouth. When I, as the pastor of the church, shared with the gentleman that he could no longer speak the words he received until his heart issues got settled, he left the church feeling that his hurt and anger were justified and validated. His motivation for receiving and speaking words from the Lord was impure.

We should desire to come to the Lord to hear from Him from a pure heart. There is one key reason that we should want to hear God's voice, and there are four "sub-reasons" we should come to the Lord desiring to listen to His voice. I will list the four "sub-reasons" first.

- We desire to know for sure that He hears our prayers
- We want to know for sure that He accepts us
- We wish to know His will and destiny for our lives
- We desire to know and experience His manifested presence

All four of those reasons are good, and there is certainly nothing wrong with them. However, the four reasons listed above has one major problem. Each idea has "us" and what "we desire" from beginning to end.

One of the hardest truths we will embrace in our Christian life is the fact that "it is not about us." The reason this is so difficult to internalize is that many of the Christian books we read, the music we listen to, and the sermons preached, starts and ends with us. Many Pastors and spiritual leaders fill today's Christianity with self-help "me-isms." But folks, being a Christian is not about me, and it is not about you, it is all about God, the King of Glory.

The Word says that if we do not praise Him, the rocks will shout out, and the trees of the fields will clap their hands. God will have a people who will worship and praise Him. It must be all about the Father from beginning to end.

> *Luke 19:38-40 ESV saying, "Blessed is the King who comes in the name of the Lord! Peace in heaven and glory in the highest!" (39) And some of the Pharisees in the crowd said to him, "Teacher, rebuke your disciples." (40) He answered, "I tell you, if these were silent, the very stones would cry out."*

> *Isaiah 55:11-12 ESV so shall my word be that goes out from my mouth; it shall not return to me empty, but it shall accomplish that which I purpose, and shall succeed in the thing for which I sent it. (12)*

"For you shall go out in joy and be led forth in peace; the mountains and the hills before you shall break forth into singing, and all the trees of the field shall clap their hands.

Psalms 98:7-9 ESV Let the sea roar, and all that fills it; the world and those who dwell in it! (8) Let the rivers clap their hands; let the hills sing for joy together (9) before the LORD, for he comes to judge the earth. He will judge the world with righteousness, and the peoples with equity.

Matthew 3:9 ESV And do not presume to say to yourselves, 'We have Abraham as our father,' for I tell you, God is able from these stones to raise up children for Abraham.

If we truly embrace and believe by faith the written Word of God, we don't need to hear God's voice to know that He loves us, hears us, and accepts us. We will identify these truths from reading the Word of God by faith. The proper motivation to hearing God's voice comes down to five keys elements that always end in God getting the glory and honor.

- ➤ We want to listen to what He says
- ➤ So that we can say what He says
- ➤ So that we can do what He does
- ➤ So that we can see what He sees
- ➤ So that we can be who He is
- ➤ So that He gets all the praise and glory

1 John 1:1-3 ESV That which was from the beginning,

which we have heard, which we have seen with our eyes, which we looked upon and have touched with our hands, concerning the word of life— (2) the life was made manifest, and we have seen it, and testify to it and proclaim to you the eternal life, which was with the Father and was made manifest to us— (3) that which we have seen and heard we proclaim also to you, so that you too may have fellowship with us; and indeed our fellowship is with the Father and with his Son Jesus Christ.

Fellowship with the Father and Son is an everyday reality for those born again through the blood of Christ. God the Father desires to have fellowship with us. God the Father wants to COMMUNE and COMMUNICATE with us in a genuine fellowship of His love and joy. This book is not a study for us to get "more of God" or "more from God," but help to commune with Abba, Father. While the preaching of today and the books that many authors write communicate self-preservation, we need to know that the Word of God says if we want to be great, we need to humble ourselves. That means we need to give our life away. Because if we're going to live, we need to die to ourselves. The way up is down.

Fellowship with God is not possible if we don't speak with Him and don't receive from Him. He talks to us through His Word, through His prophets, through dreams and visions, and through others whom the Father uses to get His message to us. However, he desires to speak directly to His children and that His children hear His voice and obey Him.

1 Corinthians 1:9 ESV God is faithful, by whom you were called into the fellowship of his Son, Jesus

> *Christ our Lord.*
>
> *Acts 4:19-20 ESV But Peter and John answered them, "Whether it is right in the sight of God to listen to you rather than to God, you must judge, (20) for we cannot but speak of what we have seen and heard."*

BEING A VOICE FOR GOD AND TO GOD

Revelation chapter 4 talks about voices proceeding from the throne. This voice proceeding from the throne is what we become when we have ears to hear. Speaking an accurate word from God is how the prophets of the Old Testament operated. They stood in the counsel of the Lord, and it burned like a fire within them, causing them to speak. When we neglect the discipline of walking in the Spirit and experiencing personal time with the Lord, we will stop talking boldly in His name.

> *Revelation 4:1 ESV After this I looked, and behold, a door standing open in heaven! And the first voice, which I had heard speaking to me like a trumpet, said, "Come up here, and I will show you what must take place after this."*

When we hear from the Lord, we can make bold proclamations to God in our prayer times concerning His Word and His love towards us. One of the benefits of hearing from the Lord is knowing with full assurance that we are at the exact right place at the exact right time in history, fulfilling the Father's perfect will. We can say to the Father, "Because I hear You;"

- I am whom You say that I am because You said it, I heard it, and I believe it.
- I can do what You say that I can do because You said it, I heard it, and I believe it.
- I have now on the earth and for all eternity what You say that I have because You said it, I heard it, and I believe it.

Each of us weathered a blasting at some point with words of discouragement from someone who thought they were doing God a favor by revealing our faults. If that is the only thing we hear, we will walk in the discouragement of hurtful and hateful words of others all of our life. If we get into the habit of hearing from the Father, we develop a two-way relationship where we receive His love and acceptance as His child.

The Father always corrects us by His love and would never blast us with hateful accusations. When we do not hear from the Father, we lend an ear to the accuser of the brothers who will scream the same allegations that some of our well-meaning friends would do. If the book of Job teaches us anything, it tells us that there are friends ready to accuse us and condemn us when we are at our lowest point.

We can find ourselves in trouble if we allow the enemy to speak an agreement to what others have said, and we give an ear to those voices. Imagine how positive and healthy the body of Christ would be if we would first read from God's Word concerning what He has said about us, and then we hear His voice in agreement with those words. Following these two spiritual exercises with us repeating to others what we have read and heard from the Father would cause us to internalize the truth of God's Word within us.

When we come under verbal attack, we need to get alone before the Father and hear Him. In doing this, we encourage ourselves in the Lord.

> *1 Samuel 30:6 ESV And David was greatly distressed, for the people spoke of stoning him, because all the people were bitter in soul, each for his sons and daughters. But David strengthened himself in the LORD his God.*

GOD'S WORD WILL JUDGE:

In these days in which we live, everyone has an opinion about moral decisions. Pastors who embrace the truths of God's Word should draw "lines in the sand" about what God says and where they stand morally on specific issues. Many people think that when God judges us, we will be judged by what we believe. That seems right. However, we are not going to be judged just by what we believe. What does the Word of God say about what will judge us?

> *John 12:47-50 ESV If anyone hears my words and does not keep them, I do not judge him; for I did not come to judge the world but to save the world. (48) The one who rejects me and does not receive my words has a judge; the word that I have spoken will judge him on the last day. (49) For I have not spoken on my own authority, but the Father who sent me has himself given me a commandment—what to say and what to speak. (50) And I know that his commandment is eternal life. What I say, therefore, I say as the Father has told me."*

The words, which the Lord spoke, will judge us on

the last day. It is not just what we believe that will judge us, it is also the words of our Lord that will judge us. Typically, when pastors and church leaders get together, they discuss what they deem as relevant and morally acceptable. There is a trap we can get into concerning the standards of morality. We start thinking that if we can get enough people to feel as we believe, then the majority is always right. The majority vote does not make something right. It is not standing on the side of the majority that will judge us. It is the words spoken by our Lord that will judge us.

Therefore, hearing from the Father is not an end in itself. We must obey and do what we hear. Hearing from the Father is not so we can run around proclaiming that we "got a word." Hearing from the Father is not something that God does so we can have the emotional experiences of goosebumps and liver shivers. Hearing from the Father is like a rudder for the ship of life. It is the Person of the Holy Spirit that illuminates God's written Word. When social and cultural situations go against God's Word and character, we need to have ears to hear what the Father is saying lest we find ourselves drawn by the amoral current of society. Hearing God becomes an anchor to our soul, allowing us to stand when no one else stands with us.

> *Hebrews 6:19 ESV We have this as a sure and steadfast anchor of the soul, a hope that enters into the inner place behind the curtain,*

Stand in God's pea patch even if you stand alone, even if the enemy outnumbers you, and also if it seems like just a dumb patch of peas. Why? Why should I stand, Pastor? For no other reason, then it is God's pea patch.

2 Samuel 23:11-12 ESV And next to him was Shammah, the son of Agee the Hararite. The Philistines gathered together at Lehi, where there was a plot of ground full of lentils, and the men fled from the Philistines. (12) But he took his stand in the midst of the plot and defended it and struck down the Philistines, and the LORD worked a great victory.

The moral standard with God has not changed throughout the entire history of humanity. Each culture and society in each generation set its ethical standards both nationally and individually, regardless of what God says. Not only does society move from an immoral position to an amoral status, but they also seek to redefine "mankind" and "sin."

There are no absolutes in an amoral society except for one, "they will do what is right in their own eyes." In this type of fast-paced amoral society, ever pressing us to conform, we can lose our identity as to who we are and whose we are. We can lose our identity as part of the body of Christ, and as a child of the King. Then we naturally take on the character of the culture or society where we live or socialize. Our Christian faith then becomes a small sub-culture that we address and give time to only on certain days and situations. Then the voice of the Father becomes nothing more than a distant echo somewhere out of our reach.

An amoral society embraces the ideals of lawlessness, often referred to in secular circles as Postmodernism. The idea of "doing what is right in our own eyes" moves society from lawlessness in behavior to being bound nationally by a spirit of lawlessness.

When we abide with the Father to hear His voice, we hear kindred reminders that we are His sons, heirs, and friends. As friends of God, we want our lives to be holy, moral, and righteous before Him. God's standard of morality should not consist of a measure derived from our friends getting together to discuss what is right or wrong in our own eyes. We know from the Word of God the standard which God declares. He declares that His rule and morals are absolute, and God is always righteous in His deeds. The Father cannot be anything but virtuous and unchanging. If we embrace the immutability of God, then we have a real anchor for our soul and a compass for our life. His voice is and will always be accurate and for our good.

> ***Hebrews 6:17-19 ESV So when God desired to show more convincingly to the heirs of the promise the unchangeable character of his purpose, he guaranteed it with an oath, (18) so that by two unchangeable things, in which it is impossible for God to lie, we who have fled for refuge might have strong encouragement to hold fast to the hope set before us. (19) We have this as a sure and steadfast anchor of the soul, a hope that enters into the inner place behind the curtain,***

The Bible reveals from the written text and from the spoken word that God is Holy. When we hear from the Father about morality, we know that we are not hearing the opinion of men but are receiving an "eternal kingdom-established" standard. When we hear from Him, we will want to honor Him in word, deed, and thought. When we hear from the Father, we can morally reflect His nature and character. If judgment comes by the words of our Lord, how important is it for us to have ears to hear the Father's words right now on this day? One would not have to read far into the Old Testament Prophets, like Jeremiah and Hosea, to see how the Word of God was words of judgment against a sinful and rebellious people who refused to repent from their ways. The Bible says this about God's Word.

> *Hebrews 4:12 ESV For the word of God is living and active, sharper than any two-edged sword, piercing to the division of soul and of spirit, of joints and of marrow, and discerning the thoughts and intentions of the heart.*
>
> *Hebrews 3:5-8 ESV Now Moses was faithful in all God's house as a servant, to testify to the things that were to be spoken later, (6) but Christ is faithful over God's house as a son. And we are his house if indeed we hold fast our confidence and our boasting in our hope. (7) Therefore, as the Holy Spirit says, "Today, if you hear his voice, (8) do not harden your hearts as in the rebellion, on the day of testing in the wilderness,*
>
> *Hebrews 5:11-14 ESV About this we have much to say, and it is hard to explain, since you have become dull of hearing. (12) For though by this time you ought to be teachers, you need someone to teach you again the basic principles of the oracles of God. You need milk, not solid food, (13) for everyone who lives on milk is unskilled in the word of righteousness, since he is a child. (14) But solid food is for the mature, for those who have their powers of discernment trained by constant practice to distinguish good from evil.*

THE HOLY SPIRIT CALLING US TO HEAR GOD'S VOICE:

Do we want to hear God's voice? If we do, we may be hearing Him already. He may be the one giving us the longing to listen to Him. God, the Holy Spirit, is speaking to us about the necessity of hearing God's voice. Anything or any desire we have for spiritual things did not start with us but from the Father. The fact that we desire to hear from the Father is a wooing of the Holy Spirit to do so. This drawing or wooing of the Person of the Holy Spirit leaves us with a decision of obeying the Holy Spirit. It will not happen if we take a passive mode. If we disobey, we are either quenching or grieving the conviction and wooing of the Holy Spirit. This disobedience can lead to the hardening of our hearts, which will hinder the future wooing of the Holy Spirit in our lives.

> *Job 33:13-17 ESV Why do you contend against him, saying, 'He will answer none of man's words'? (14) For God speaks in one way, and in two, though man does not perceive it. (15) In a dream, in a vision of the night, when deep sleep falls on men, while they slumber on their beds, (16) then he opens the ears of men and terrifies them with warnings, (17) that he may turn man aside from his deed and conceal pride from a man;*

> *James 1:17 ESV Every good gift and every perfect gift is from above, coming down from the Father of lights with whom there is no variation or shadow due to change.*

> *1 Thessalonians 5:19 ESV (19) Do not quench the Spirit.*

> *Ephesians 4:30 ESV And do not grieve the Holy Spirit of God, by whom you were sealed for the day of redemption.*

Ever wonder why at times, God is so mysterious and seemingly distant? Ever wonder why at times, the Bible takes so long to read? It is simple. God is looking for those who are interested in pursuing Him. There is an old saying which many of us have used concerning Christian discipleship. "If it were easy, every Christian would do it." Taken from the Book of Job, "Does he love you for nothing?" How important is it to hear from the Father? It is for the ones who have ears to listen to God, who will receive the truths of God's treasures.

> *Revelation 2:7 ESV He who has an ear, let him hear what the Spirit says to the churches. To the one who conquers I will grant to eat of the tree of life, which is in the paradise of God.'*

> *Revelation 2:11 ESV He who has an ear, let him hear what the Spirit says to the churches. The one who conquers will not be hurt by the second death.'*

> *Revelation 2:17 ESV He who has an ear, let him hear what the Spirit says to the churches. To the one who conquers I will give some of the hidden manna, and I will give him a white stone, with a new name written on the stone that no one knows except the one who receives it.'*

We must come to the Lord on His terms and for His purposes. We can certainly come to Him with our needs, but for some believers, that is all they seem to do. We all desire to have our needs met. This is not a statement meant to condemn us but to encourage us to speak with the Father in the good times also. We should be ready to receive from the Lord in the good times as well as in times of crisis. Some of us have had friends who were needy all the time. Some of us have had friends who were just interested in what we could do for them. Those are hardly friends, and it is a complicated relationship at best. As a pastor, we called these types of believers "high maintenance church members." They don't desire to bring their gifts, talents, and fellowship to the church to share because they typically are takers. Is that how we treat God? God wants us to share so much more of ourselves with Him. The Father wants us to share our joys, our dreams, our failures, and all that pertains to us. In doing so, we must remember that God has things to say to us. Many times, He wants us to listen to His voice.

7

THE JOY OF EXPERIENCING GOD'S VOICE

I have dedicated Chapter 7 to Artur Mironichenko, who believed the joy we experience in knowing God's voice was a needed addition in this book. Artur corroborated with me in writing the material of this chapter.

Our coming to Him and hearing His voice should be to know Him more. The Father hides things in His heart, which can only be found by those who genuinely seek Him. Finding the Father's heart is the highest form of pleasure that a human being can experience. Yes, the quest may often seem challenging and, at times, dry, but that is typical because we don't know Him for who He truly is until we find His grace in the wilderness place.

> *Song of Solomon 1:2 ESV She Let him kiss me with the kisses of his mouth! For your love is better than wine;*

The Song of Solomon is two-fold in its message. The first is an actual account of a romance between the King and the poor, yet beautiful Shulamite woman. The second is a typology picturing Christ to the church (the believers). She (the church) cried out to the King (Christ), asking Him to kiss her. She states that the love of Christ for the church is better than wine, meaning it is intoxicating.

HIDE AND SEEK

Most of us can remember the joy of playing hide-and-seek as a child or with our children. At the sight of disappearing behind a corner, the little ones counting would sometimes cry. Realizing that the one counting was crying, we would make ourselves visible where we were hiding by sticking out a hand and calling out His name. If that does not catch His attention, we would jump out from behind the corner, wait for him to see us, and then we would run and hide in the same place again. Usually, he would easily crawl to where we hid and pretended to find us. The union makes us all laugh and enjoy each other's company all the more.

We will find the same applies to God, our heavenly Father. He often plays hide and seek yet wants to be perceived and seen by us. He wants to be known by us. He leaves evidence of His presence in nature, through different circumstances, through the community, or in the happy moment of His real and tangible touch. Once we experience this joy of finding His presence, we will find ourselves seeking out moments with Him to be with Him. Knowing that there are pleasures evermore at His right hand should encourage us deeply. Job realized that God plays hide and seek. Even when Job could not see or feel God, he rested in the calm assurance that the Father's eyes were always on him.

> *Job 23:8-14 ESV "Behold, I go forward, but he is not there, and backward, but I do not perceive him; (9) on the left hand when he is working, I do not behold him; he turns to the right hand, but I do not see him. (10) But he knows the way that I take; when he has tried me, I shall come out as gold. (11) My foot has*

held fast to his steps; I have kept his way and have not turned aside. (12) I have not departed from the commandment of his lips; I have treasured the words of his mouth more than my portion of food. (13) But he is unchangeable, and who can turn him back? What he desires, that he does. (14) For he will complete what he appoints for me, and many such things are in his mind.

What are some of the things we can expect when we hear the voice of Father? To know Him is to know His heart. He may give us direction to impact a people group and equip us with love to do so. The Holy Spirit may speak to us about the offense in our hearts and lead us towards reconciliation and restoration. All the while, through various circumstances, He refines our faith and love. The result is that we grow up in the knowledge of Him. The end goal is not to have a bigger or better ministry, bring a good sermon, or to "wow" people with our ability to hear God. One of my favorite sayings that I picked up in 1989 at Park Avenue Baptist Church in Titusville, Florida, from Pastor Peter Lord is that we are "To begin with the end in mind." The ultimate goal of hearing the voice of the Father is an actual deep relationship with Jesus that produces a continual desire to know Him more.

Each time the Spirit of wisdom and revelation gets a hold of us and reveals the depth of the knowledge of Christ, we experience in our character a slow transformation into the image of Christ. The outward impact is that natural fruit will come from our lives. We will release the Word of God in the Spirit of truth.

KEY STATEMENT: We cannot separate God's presence from His voice.

He speaks. Throughout life, when God speaks in any of His ways, we can enjoy growing in the knowledge of who He is. His personality and character are always part of His voice because it comes out of Him.

We need to ask ourselves, "What is our focus that captures the majority of our time and resources?" This focus could be our jobs, our health, our hobbies, our possessions, our religious activities, or our families. We need to have God and His presence as our focus.

Let's say we have the focus of our attention down to two things, hearing God's voice and having God's manifested presence. So, the question arises, "Are we focusing on just hearing God's voice or on God Himself?" It is to the level that we set our eyes on Him that we begin to explore the depths of who He is and who is really speaking to us. Our Lord said that "My sheep hear my voice." The key here is being like sheep, who know, who follow, and who trust the shepherd. When the sheep grow in a relationship with the shepherd, the recognizing of His voice naturally follows. We need to incline our ears and take delight in the Lord as we grow to know Him more.

> ***Psalms 16:11 ESV You make known to me the path of life; in your presence there is fullness of joy; at your right hand are pleasures forevermore.***

HIS VOICE MEANS HIS PRESENCE

When the Father speaks, we do not just experience pleasure from an emotional release, but we take pleasure in the revelation of the character and nature of God. His voice is not there to give us a command or lead us in our meaningful choices. It is for fellowship, communion, and the enjoyment of knowing who He is. The voice we hear comes forth from Him, the Creator. What are you saying, Charles? We are to first and foremost focus our attention and seek after God and His heart, and then the hearing of His voice will be a natural outcome. Yes, I have seen those who want to hear God's voice for the "hearing sake" to "get a word" and yet not focused on the presence of the One speaking. Why is it we place so much emphasis on the supernatural over the Savior? And so much importance over and the gift and not the giver? Too many desire "God's power over His presence." ***We are a "called-out" people meant for His Presence.***

The experience of His voice should always be an enjoying experience for our souls. When we truly have His voice, we have His presence. The Father created us to hear from Him and obey Him. He speaks words of tender kindness to us. Even when the sound we hear is a correction or verbal chastisement, it is a revelation of the Father's loving attention and discipline. When God disciplines us, we can take joy in the fact that we are true sons of God. A seven-month-old son smiles with satisfaction when he hears the voice of his Father. He receives a blessing from just hearing his Father's love for him.

David said in the Psalms that there was one main thing that he desired. Think about it: David, a man surrounded by fame, fortune, relationships, power, and honor. Yet there was only one thing he desired. He enjoyed being with the Lord and made that desire his most significant priority. God spoke to him and entrusted him with words that today we embrace as Holy Scripture.

Psalms 27:4 ESV One thing have I asked of the

LORD, that will I seek after: that I may dwell in the house of the LORD all the days of my life, to gaze upon the beauty of the LORD and to inquire in his temple.

In Psalms 81 David is speaking from God's perspective of Israel, failing to listen to His voice. God gives them over to their stubbornness, but His ultimate desire for Israel is that she would turn and listen to Him. He concludes by saying He would feed them with the finest of wheat and with honey from the rock. This feeding is the sweetness of His voice that satisfies our whole being. When we listen, His words penetrate us to the core, and we are fully satisfied in Him.

Psalms 81:10-13 ESV I am the LORD your God, who brought you up out of the land of Egypt. Open your mouth wide, and I will fill it. (11) "But my people did not listen to my voice; Israel would not submit to me. (12) So I gave them over to their stubborn hearts, to follow their own counsels. (13) Oh, that my people would listen to me, that Israel would walk in my ways!

Psalms 81:16 ESV But he would feed you with the finest of the wheat, and with honey from the rock I would satisfy you."

We need to maintain awareness that the nature of God as our Father, teacher, friend, husband, pastor, counselor, King, ambassador, and Savior, all point to relationship and fellowship. A relationship without a genuine connection is not reality. The Father wants to reveal Himself to us so that we would know Him intimately. There is a pleasure to experience as we grow in relationship with all aspects of the nature of God. In moments of a deep heart-to-heart conversation with the Lord or sitting and waiting on the Lord, there is a deep joy to be found in His presence. There will be times when little or nothing at all will be "spoken," but communication will still be going on. The knowledge of having His manifested presence as we pray brings the peace and rest of God to our hearts.

As a married man, do I love how my wife makes me feel and the things she does for me, or do I love who she is inside out? Of course, I should enjoy all the things my wife does for me, and I love how she makes me feel; however, first and foremost, I genuinely love who she is as a person. As husbands, we should experience our wives with all five of our senses. For instance, we have the joy of loving our wife's voice. She could be either singing or whispering, and when we hear her voice, it should cause our heart to leap. However, our wives are more to us than the sound of their voice. The woman's voice reveals who she is, and it invites us to know her more personally. That is the same with the Lord. God is more than His voice. Knowing how to hear the Father's voice brings us into deep fellowship and enjoyment of God. There is joy unspeakable and full of glory to be found in His presence. Therefore, we seek to hear His voice in as many ways as possible. Speak Lord, the servants of God are listening!

> *1 Peter 1:8 ESV Though you have not seen him, you love him. Though you do not now see him, you believe in him and rejoice with joy that is inexpressible and filled with glory,*

> *1 Samuel 3:8-10 ESV And the LORD called Samuel again the third time. And he arose and went to Eli*

and said, "Here I am, for you called me." Then Eli perceived that the LORD was calling the boy. (9) Therefore Eli said to Samuel, "Go, lie down, and if he calls you, you shall say, 'Speak, LORD, for your servant hears.'" So Samuel went and lay down in his place. (10) And the LORD came and stood, calling as at other times, "Samuel! Samuel!" And Samuel said, "Speak, for your servant hears."

8

GETTING OURSELVES SPIRITUALLY READY: THE WILLING HEART

In September 1974, after accepting Christ as Savior, I walked around the military base with my right hand extended as if our Lord Jesus Christ was holding it and leading each step of the way. Remembering back to that first week in September 1974, I had a full page of appointments that required signatures as I was out-processing from one military base to relocate to Germany. Not owning a car, I found it necessary to walk to every required location in acquire my needed signature. The Air Force base I was signing out from was enormous, and the essential places I had to visit to attain the out-processing names were scattered all over the military installation. Each site visited required the NCOIC (Non-Commission Officer in Charge) available to sign the discharge paperwork. Because of the number of signatures needed, the problematic locating all of the NCOIC's to complete the necessary signatures, and the size of the base, the Commander gave us one full week off from work to complete the out-processing paperwork.

Having prayed, our Lord guided me each step of the way. Having the right order of signatures was necessary, which could not be out of sequence. As a new believer, I was learning to trust God for guidance in the small and simple things of life. Throughout the day, I felt God's nudge, and His voice was clear as He spoke and guided me step-by-step around the military installation. Every place I entered had the NCOIC present so that the paperwork could be signed.

What usually would have required a week's worth of work in attaining the needed signatures ended up requiring about five hours' worth of effort. It was a great training time in learning to hear and trust the voice of the Father and the leadership of the Holy Spirit.

It has been over forty years since that first experience of having the Holy Spirit's guidance around that military base for signatures. His presence is just as real today as it was forty years ago. I not only have the testimonies of supernatural "God encounters" from forty years ago but fresh daily encounters as I hear and obey. He still leads me by that still small voice. The presence and reality of God's leadership today is as real and vibrant as it was forty-plus years ago. Praise God, for His mercy endures forever.

THE KEY TO THE KEYS

In 2014, some dear Christian friends from Germany came to visit and stay in our home. They had scheduled to leave our home the same day Debby and I had a necessary appointment we had to attend. We told our dear friends goodbye, and we left our house first to make our appointment. Our German friends were to lock up the house when they left. A couple of hours later, our German friends called to inform us that they had lost their car keys and could not go anywhere. When we returned home a few hours later, our German friends were still looking for their lost car keys. After questioning them about the places they had searched and any places they still needed to explore, we all felt a sense of hopelessness, not knowing what to do next. Our friends informed us that they had been searching through every place in the house at least four times.

PREPARING OURSELVES TO HEAR GOD'S VOICE

We all were sitting together in the living room, thinking about our next step in acquiring new car keys. Mark, one of the German brothers, began reading something from a book relating to their current situation. The first chapter in the book was titled "The Lost Keys." How ironic. As Mark read aloud from the book, we all listened intently. In the middle of his reading, another voice spoke out loudly in my inner ear. It was a clear message from God the Holy Spirit coming forth supernaturally. The word spoken to me was a "matter of fact word." The Holy Spirit spoke and told me to place my left hand down deep into the left side of the big leather chair in which I was sitting. Obeying our Lord's command, I thrust my left hand down into the chair and immediately hooked a key ring. With a quick pull, their lost keys popped out the side of the chair in front of everyone as Mark was finishing the chapter on "The Lost Keys." It was a great testimony of the Holy Spirit's leadership and how the Father has an answer to our every need if only we listen to His voice.

If we wanted to run in a race, we certainly wouldn't wait until the day of the race to go out and run. We would naturally spend weeks or months preparing ourselves physically and mentally for the contest so that we wouldn't injure ourselves and so we would be able to run a good race. The training would also enable us to compete against others and help us complete the race correctly.

Think for a minute about the things in which we say and do. This next sentence is a crucial statement worthy of our attention.

Many things we do today, coming from habits and impulse, were things we had to learn, sometimes by trial and error.

The same is true with hearing the voice of the Father. There are things we need to prepare to be less involved with this temporal world and more involved with the eternal matters of the Kingdom of God. This idea of preparation brings me to another truth that we need to wrap our minds around. Hearing the voice of God is a supernatural event that has the eternal kingdom of God as it's motivation.

KEY POINT: The primary purpose and work of the Holy Spirit are to take us to and reveal the Son, our Lord Jesus Christ. The primary purpose of the Son is to take us to and show us the Father. The primary purpose of the Father is to prepare for Himself His inheritance, which is us. So, when we hear from God the Father, God the Holy Spirit, and God the Son, know that all of the Godhead is involved, and the Kingdom of God is the motivation of the Father preparing a people for Himself.

We know that things would seem a lot easier if God just shouted out our name and instructions in a booming voice, which unmistakably came from the throne room of heaven. It would be like sitting in a hospital waiting room where the TV was blasting over a noise-filled place full of chatting patients. Then suddenly, our name is called over the loudspeaker, telling us which room the doctor will see us in. The volume of the speaker drowns out both the noise of the TV and the room full of people. The directions heard were clear and precise. We knew the command was specifically for us and nobody else in the waiting room.

Goodness, wouldn't this be easy if God spoke this way all the time? No matter what voices we were listening to, or who had our attention, we had the assurance that God would interrupt with a loud blasting voice over all other sounds with His clear and precise commands. We would never have to say, "I don't know what God wants me to do." Biblically speaking, we find examples of God speaking loudly in thunder. These, however, were isolated events and not the norm in the way He speaks to us. Elijah had trained his ears to hear the still small voice of the Father. In 1 Kings 19:12, it says that God spoke in a low whisper.

> *1 Kings 19:11-13 ESV And he said, "Go out and stand on the mount before the LORD." And behold, the LORD passed by, and a great and strong wind tore the mountains and broke in pieces the rocks before the LORD, but the LORD was not in the wind. And after the wind an earthquake, but the LORD was not in the earthquake. (12) And after the earthquake a fire, but the LORD was not in the fire. And after the fire the sound of a low whisper. (13) And when Elijah heard it, he wrapped his face in his cloak and went out and stood at the entrance of the cave. And behold, there came a voice to him and said, "What are you doing here, Elijah?"*

When we are dealing with hearing from the Lord, we must get over the insecurity or fear of not knowing if the voice we hear is God. This fear of uncertainty can cause spiritual and mental paralysis that will keep us from seeking to hear, speaking forth what we hear, or walking out what we hear.

The five keys areas in which we must prepare ourselves to be a believer with a willing heart to hear God are;

- ➢ We must be sure that we are born again
- ➢ We must give and receive forgiveness

- We must have an attitude of submission
- We must stand in faith
- We must ask, seek and knock

FIRST: WE MUST BE BORN AGAIN:

Understand that first and foremost, we must be born again to hear God's voice regularly as a child. The need for salvation does not exclude God from speaking to spiritually lost people. When He does, however, it is usually from a position of solemn warning.

God, as a Father, speaks to His children. His children are only those who have been born again. We all need to be saved or spiritually born again. To be born again is not about getting baptized in water, joining a church, or maintaining a creed or doctrine filled with a list of sacraments. Being saved is also not having a mental assent about God. Even the demons believe in God, the Father, the Son, and the Holy Spirit.

Being born again is realizing that our separation from God is because of sin and our sin nature. We must ask God to save us by receiving the work of grace from our Lord Jesus Christ. We are to call out by faith on the Lord for the salvation of our whole person, body, soul, and spirit. That act of faith brings about the ministry of reconciliation and adoption, whereby we experience passage into the family of God. One incredible benefit of adoption into God's family is the open door where we can converse with God the Father. We have the spiritual authority and position to hear His voice because we are now His adopted children.

There are no "good" people. Some people do good moral things, but according to the Word of God, there are no "good" people. Doing good things may make someone ethical, but it does not make them good. The Jews knew that one would only use the term "good" for God and His actions.

> *Romans 3:10-12 ESV as it is written: "None is righteous, no, not one; (11) no one understands; no one seeks for God. (12) All have turned aside; together they have become worthless; no one does good, not even one."*

> *Luke 18:18-19 ESV And a ruler asked him, "Good Teacher, what must I do to inherit eternal life?" (19) And Jesus said to him, "Why do you call me good? No one is good except God alone.*

Here is one of those critical statements in which we need to remember. Everyone is a sinner. We sin because we are sinners. **We do not become sinners because we sin; we sin because we are sinners.** The fact that we are sinners by nature means that we cannot come to God on our merit. The fact that we are sinners leads to four critical statements, which we should remember when soul winning.

1. We are separated from God because He is holy, and we are not.
2. We can come to God only through His Son, the Lord Jesus Christ.
3. We cannot come by merit to earn salvation.
4. We come to God as we are and receive His gift of salvation as a work of grace. The word grace means "unmerited or unearned favor."

> *Romans 3:23-24 ESV for all have sinned and fall short of the glory of God, (24) and are justified by*

his grace as a gift, through the redemption that is in Christ Jesus,

A lost sinner. How does this affect the sinner hearing God and God hearing the sinner?

Psalms 66:18 ESV If I had cherished iniquity in my heart, the Lord would not have listened.

The Father does not wait until we stop sinning before He saves us. He takes us as we are and forgives us and cleanses us.

Romans 5:8 ESV but God shows his love for us in that while we were still sinners, Christ died for us.

Because we are sinners, we have a wage to pay, and that wage is death. This debt or wage we need to pay means that if we refuse to receive the salvation gift of our Lord Jesus Christ, we will die in our sins and spend eternity in hell with the demons, forever separated from God. The gift of God is eternal life through our Lord Jesus Christ.

Romans 6:23 ESV For the wages of sin is death, but the free gift of God is eternal life in Christ Jesus our Lord.

The process whereby we may become a Christian is confession with the mouth and believing in the heart by faith. We need to remember that "prayers do not save people," and "works do not save people." Jesus saves people. Many will pray a prayer and still stay in a spiritually lost condition because they did not mix the prayer with a heart of faith.

Ephesians 2:8-9 ESV For by grace you have been saved through faith. And this is not your own doing; it is the gift of God, (9) not a result of works, so that no one may boast.

Romans 10:9-10 ESV because, if you confess with your mouth that Jesus is Lord and believe in your heart that God raised him from the dead, you will be saved. (10) For with the heart one believes and is justified, and with the mouth one confesses and is saved.

Hebrews 4:2 ESV For good news came to us just as to them, but the message they heard did not benefit them, because they were not united by faith with those who listened.

If we call out to God, with a heart of faith, we will experience true salvation.

Romans 10:13 ESV For "everyone who calls on the name of the Lord will be saved."

The work of salvation cannot add with it human effort or social actions. We cannot be baptized enough, give enough money, pray enough, or help our neighbor enough to earn salvation. If we could earn salvation through works or some form of human effort, then we would not need the cross of our Lord Jesus Christ. If we could save ourselves through our works, then we would be able to boast in heaven for our part in our salvation. It also means that our Lord Jesus Christ died in vain.

Ephesians 2:8-9 ESV For by grace you have been saved through faith. And this is not your own doing; it is the gift of God, (9) not a result of works, so that no one may boast.

Galatians 2:21 ESV I do not nullify the grace of God, for if righteousness were through the law, then Christ died for no purpose.

If we called on the name of our Lord Jesus Christ with a heart of faith and gave Him our life and we took on His presence, then we are not only saved, but we have become sons of God.

John 1:12 ESV But to all who did receive him, who believed in his name, he gave the right to become children of God,

Romans 8:15 ESV For you did not receive the spirit of slavery to fall back into fear, but you have received the Spirit of adoption as sons, by whom we cry, "Abba! Father!"

SECONDLY: GIVE AND RECEIVE FORGIVENESS:

Cleanse ourselves first. Ask for forgiveness and be sure that we don't hold anyone in a position of unforgiveness. We cannot expect God to speak to us if we are actively engaged in sin, especially the sin of unforgiveness. As believers, we have a relationship with the Father, but we need to maintain fellowship with the Father and not grieve the Person of the Holy Spirit.

1 John 1:7-9 ESV But if we walk in the light, as he is

in the light, we have fellowship with one another, and the blood of Jesus his Son cleanses us from all sin. (8) If we say we have no sin, we deceive ourselves, and the truth is not in us. (9) If we confess our sins, he is faithful and just to forgive us our sins and to cleanse us from all unrighteousness.

Psalms 66:18-20 ESV If I had cherished iniquity in my heart, the Lord would not have listened. (19) But truly God has listened; he has attended to the voice of my prayer. (20) Blessed be God, because he has not rejected my prayer or removed his steadfast love from me!

THIRDLY: ATTITUDE OF SUBMISSION:

We need to maintain an attitude of submission. God is God, and we are not. He knows what He is doing, even when it doesn't seem like it to us. God can always be trusted.

Ephesians 5:18-21 ESV And do not get drunk with wine, for that is debauchery, but be filled with the Spirit, (19) addressing one another in psalms and hymns and spiritual songs, singing and making melody to the Lord with your heart, (20) giving thanks always and for everything to God the Father in the name of our Lord Jesus Christ, (21) submitting to one another out of reverence for Christ.

Romans 6:16-17 ESV Do you not know that if you present yourselves to anyone as obedient slaves, you are slaves of the one whom you obey, either of sin, which leads to death, or of obedience, which leads to righteousness? (17) But thanks be to God, that you who were once slaves of sin have become obedient from the heart to the standard of teaching to which you were committed,

FOURTHLY: STAND IN FAITH:

We must have faith that God will speak to us and is speaking to us. We need to make a deliberate decision that once we hear His voice, we will also obey and follow it.

1 Corinthians 16:13 ESV (13) Be watchful, stand firm in the faith, act like men, be strong.

1 Thessalonians 3:7-8 ESV (7) for this reason, brothers, in all our distress and affliction we have been comforted about you through your faith. (8) For now we live, if you are standing fast in the Lord.

Philippians 1:27 ESV Only let your manner of life be worthy of the gospel of Christ, so that whether I come and see you or am absent, I may hear of you that you are standing firm in one spirit, with one mind striving side by side for the faith of the gospel,

Ephesians 6:11-14 ESV Put on the whole armor of God, that you may be able to stand against the schemes of the devil. (12) For we do not wrestle against flesh and blood, but against the rulers, against the authorities, against the cosmic powers over this present darkness, against the spiritual forces of evil in the heavenly places. (13) Therefore take up the whole armor of God, that you may be able to withstand in the evil day, and having done all, to stand firm. (14) Stand therefore, having fastened on the belt of truth, and having put on the breastplate of righteousness,

2 Corinthians 1:24 ESV Not that we lord it over your faith, but we work with you for your joy, for you stand firm in your faith.

FIFTHLY: ASK, SEEK, AND KNOCK:

Now comes the time to call on God and to seek God for the things we desire from Him. Knock on His door of opportunity, and He will open the door. It is essential to ask, seek, and knock in faith and not be double-minded. The Scriptures tell us that a double-minded man is unstable in all his ways and will receive nothing from the Lord.

Matthew 7:7-8 ESV "Ask, and it will be given to you; seek, and you will find; knock, and it will be opened to you. (8) For everyone who asks receives, and the one who seeks finds, and to the one who knocks it will be opened.

James 1:5-8 ESV If any of you lacks wisdom, let him ask God, who gives generously to all without reproach, and it will be given him. (6) But let him ask in faith, with no doubting, for the one who doubts is like a wave of the sea that is driven and tossed by the wind. (7) For that person must not suppose that he will receive anything from the Lord; (8) he is a double-minded man, unstable in all his ways.

9

DEVELOPING SPIRITUAL EARS TO HEAR

By now, we should know the importance of hearing the voice of God, but in practical terms, how do we develop spiritual ears to hear? Let's get into the "hearing" verses of God's Word and see what He says about having ears to hear. In the Gospels, our Lord spoke some critical phrases concerning our listening to the words of the Father. These are for our benefit as we develop ears to hear.

> *Mark 4:23-25 ESV If anyone has ears to hear, let him hear." (24) And he said to them, "Pay attention to what you hear: with the measure you use, it will be measured to you, and still more will be added to you. (25) For to the one who has, more will be given, and from the one who has not, even what he has will be taken away."*

This Mark 4:23-25 passage reveals that we need spiritual ears to hear. The phrase "let him hear" is essential because it is stating that we need to have the desire to listen to God. The slogan "let him hear" in the Greek means "to give an audience to willfully." We need to prepare ourselves that we would be an audience to God so that we can hear when He speaks.

I have Pastored churches that I longed to hear just one person say that they got a specific new word from God. I would have been happy if someone said that they had a deep desire to hear from God. Oh, dear Christian brothers and sisters, have we become so content with our little programmed Sunday morning and evening services that we don't need God to come in and disrupt anything or anyone?

There must be a desire going on deep within us that says to the Father, "I want to hear from You." When we pray this heart desire to the Father, we must make time for it to happen. In other words, we must be intentional and purpose within ourselves to do whatever it takes to listen to the voice of the Father. To be deliberate means that we take the time to do so. Hearing God is not an end in itself. The Father already knows if we have the heart to obey.

Some of us who are older can remember when our children were younger and given daily chores to do. First, we had to get their attention and communicate what we wanted them to accomplish and have them repeat the chore list back to us. We, as parents, wanted to know what they heard and if they understood our words. What if our children did not do what we asked them to do? Let's suppose that when we called them in to ask why they disobeyed, they looked at us with surprise. Let's imagine that our children would say, "But Dad, we heard you loud and clear." "that, it was a joy hearing your voice, thank you for speaking to us." Of course, we would bring the conversation back to why they didn't do what we asked of them. What if they responded, "Dad, we didn't know that you were serious about us doing anything?" "We thought you just wanted us to hear what you were saying."

This "hearing without doing" is an extreme example, but in many ways, it is how some of us operate with the Father. We think that all He wants is for us to hear Him without a thought that we need to obey His words. Again, the keyword is "hearken," which means to listen with the full intent to follow. I can't remember how many times I've heard someone stand and give a testimony about receiving a word from God from one of the 15 ways in which God speaks. However, I can count on one hand, those who took it serious enough to set out in obedience to the words which they received.

OUR OVERCOMING THE "PRACTICAL ATHEISTS" SYNDROME:

When describing some believers, we might be able to use the term "practical atheists." These people are Christians, but they live each day as though God does not exist. They make their daily decisions without prayer, biblical counsel, or having God and His kingdom in mind. The same idea goes with the prospect of hearing God. We cannot live our Christian life in word, deed, and thought as though God does not care and does not want to speak into the situation. We must develop the mindset of purposefully and intentionally giving our attention to God. We must establish selective hearing towards God and His voice with the full intent to obey.

Another aspect of living life like "practical atheists" is being prideful. We could miss God speaking because of pride. When we are puffed up or prideful, we might very well miss God speaking. What happens if someone whom we would consider to be among the "unlikely to receive a word from God" lists, gives us a "thus says the Lord?" Even Paul, when he was speaking about eating certain foods, revealed that we do not know everything and to be careful in being puffed up with what knowledge we do have.

PREPARING OURSELVES TO HEAR GOD'S VOICE

1 Corinthians 8:1-3 ESV (1) Now concerning food offered to idols: we know that "all of us possess knowledge." This "knowledge" puffs up, but love builds up. (2) If anyone imagines that he knows something, he does not yet know as he ought to know. (3) But if anyone loves God, he is known by God.

Philippians 3:15-16 ESV (15) Let those of us who are mature think this way, and if in anything you think otherwise, God will reveal that also to you. (16) Only let us hold true to what we have attained.

We all know what selective listening is. Selective listening means that we only hear what we want to hear. Careful listening is a way of describing the tendency of some to ignore things they do not want to hear. It is not a physiological condition because their ears are physically picking up sound waves resulting in hearing the words. "Selective listening" is when the mind chooses not to acknowledge the spoken words. It is not always an ongoing attempt to ignore the speech. Selective listening is a selective inattention done consciously or subconsciously.

Even the disciples of our Lord Jesus Christ had selective listening. Because of the circumstances of the week, two of the disciples walked with the resurrected Lord without recognizing Him. These men had been with our Lord Jesus Christ daily for over three years. There could have been many reasons why they could not hear Him, but the most significant reason was that the message came in a way they were unaccustomed. They did not recognize His resurrected body. Therefore, they didn't hear and understand the words He spoke to them. The words of our Lord burned within them. However, because the messenger of the talks was different in appearance, they couldn't hear His words. We typically expect God to speak to us only in a method that is familiar and accustomed to our church doctrine. If He was using a different way to express, we might find ourselves missing an excellent encounter with the Father. God, shock us with the unfamiliar and pour out a "suddenly" upon us.

> *Luke 24:13-15 ESV That very day two of them were going to a village named Emmaus, about seven miles from Jerusalem, (14) and they were talking with each other about all these things that had happened. (15) While they were talking and discussing together, Jesus himself drew near and went with them.*

> *Luke 24:27-32 ESV And beginning with Moses and all the Prophets, he interpreted to them in all the Scriptures the things concerning himself. (28) So they drew near to the village to which they were going. He acted as if he were going farther, (29) but they urged him strongly, saying, "Stay with us, for it is toward evening and the day is now far spent." So he went in to stay with them. (30) When he was at table with them, he took the bread and blessed and broke it and gave it to them. (31) And their eyes were opened, and they recognized him. And he vanished from their sight. (32) They said to each other, "Did not our hearts burn within us while he talked to us on the road, while he opened to us the Scriptures?"*

HEARING WHAT WE WANT TO HEAR

Typically, men get accused of having selective listening, especially towards their wives and children.

Careful listening is frequent everyday interaction. People hear what they want to hear and tune out the things they don't want to hear. It all comes down to giving attention to those things found to be of interest or importance.

Growing up in a small town in Augusta County, Virginia, was indeed a blessing, and for sure, exemplified the simple life. Our family lived close to the railroad tracks. Who didn't love the sound of trains coming through town and blowing their whistles? To me, the loud bellowing of a train whistle represented a sense of freedom. As children, many of us would imagine ourselves jumping on one of those trains, riding it to wherever, and living the life of a hobo.

It seemed natural to tune one's ears to the sound of the train whistle because of being emotionally and mentally linked to it. A few years ago, my wife and I lived in a community south of Greensboro, North Carolina. One of our first experiences upon moving there was hearing the whistle of the city train in the distance. Many of our friends around us had not listened to the blow of train whistle for years because they have learned to filter it out. Each day, especially in the early mornings, I looked forward to that train whistle. That long, low whistle caused my mind to be flooded over with childhood memories. Once again, even over 65 years old, the train whistle stirred the desire to jump that train and go wherever those wheels rolled. Funny, a preacher by God's calling and a nomadic hobo by heart.

It's easy to draw our attention to something like the sound of a train whistle. In doing so, we give an ear to hear its musical sound. We can tune into the noise of the whistle while tuning out all other noises that interfere with it. Today, many of us stay tuned into the sound of our cell phones. A few months past I was in a waiting room at a

Veterans hospital. Imagine a large room crowded with people and each person having a phone. I watched with humor when someone's phone rang. When that incoming call rang, almost everyone in the waiting room picked up their phone to see if they have a call, even if they knew it wasn't their ring tone. We have been programmed and conditioned by our cell phone use that the sound of any ring tone is all we need to check our phones.

We give considerable time and attention to those things which we are interested in physically, mentally, or emotionally. It is of no surprise that the degree of consideration in which we provide a person or an item can shift radically. This level of engrossment can be based on the interest of the subject, the current circumstances, or having a mental, emotional, physical, relational, or spiritual bond to it. Certain people, electronic gadgets, or topics in our life command our complete attention, while others we find annoying. Those items in which we have little interest will find it nearly impossible to compete for our attention.

It is disturbing how much our cell phones are dominating most of our daily attention. The fast-paced technological and digital world we live in today makes focusing our attention difficult because a flood of information constantly bombards us. The assimilation of all the information overload that is going on around us today is impossible. Therefore, we rely on selective listening so that we do not suffer from information overload. We also have developed an information scan that goes over a multitude of data each second to spot that one thing that might be of interest. The attention span of our younger generation is now less than a second. They are honed-in on the massive data flow, and only the spectacular and acute gains the right to their attention.

That is why this new wave of churches are using modern media to draw in young believers and keep their attention. To cope in this fast-moving society, we consciously or subconsciously shut out things that our brains deem as unimportant or unrelated to our current situation. Unfortunately, it seems that our youngest generation would only hear God if He zooms in with a wave of lightning strobing the sky in a maze of colors, thunder blasting a rhythmic bass beat, and the cold rain dancing across the tin roof of the church. Otherwise, it's mundane and boring.

SELECTIVE LISTENING AND HEARING GOD:

What does selective listening have to do with hearing God? If we already have information overload or feel "burdened down," we tend to consciously or subconsciously reject any other input that is going to add to our mental, emotional, or physical state and well-being. Either by being taught or from personal experience we know that when we hear from God, there is typically a response from us demanding an action or change. Many times, we don't want the added emotional and mental stress of trying to be obedient to God's voice when so many other voices are making demands on us; therefore, we hit the "delete" button.

The attitude that hearing God could be another burden or added stress is a belief that does not come from God. He is not a burden and always desires the best for us. He knows us, our current situations and needs, far more thoroughly than we could even imagine. As we look again at the passage in Mark 4:23, we see that we need to desire to hear from the Father. There must be an honest desire within us to hear God's voice.

> *Mark 4:23 ESV If anyone has ears to hear, let him hear."*

When I say that we need an honest desire within us to hear God's voice, we are speaking about a passion that comes from our soulish man. The soul is made up of our mind (how we think), our emotions (how we feel), and our will (how we choose). Because we have the Person of the Holy Spirit dwelling within our spirit, there is a supernatural desire in our spirit-man to stay in communion and communication with the Father. The Holy Spirit within us is in constant intercession with the Father.

> *Romans 8:15-16 ESV For you did not receive the spirit of slavery to fall back into fear, but you have received the Spirit of adoption as sons, by whom we cry, "Abba! Father!" (16) The Spirit himself bears witness with our spirit that we are children of God,*

> *Romans 8:26 ESV Likewise the Spirit helps us in our weakness. For we do not know what to pray for as we ought, but the Spirit himself intercedes for us with groanings too deep for words.*

> *2 Corinthians 13:14 ESV (14) The grace of the Lord Jesus Christ and the love of God and the fellowship of the Holy Spirit be with you all.*

SEEKING TO HEAR GOD'S VOICE REQUIRES YOUR UNDIVIDED ATTENTION

It is not an option to hear the voice of God. Hearing God's voice is both a mandate and evidence of being a follower of our Lord.

> *Mark 4:23 ESV If anyone has ears to hear, let him hear."*

As men, when we watch television, we tend to zero in on the movie or the football game or whatever. Our wives could be standing next to us saying something, and typically we would be very oblivious to it. During these times, when we focus our attention on what we are watching, her voice would be nothing more than, at best, a background noise. Ladies, this is not meant to be mean; it is just the way some men operate. It is not that we do not love our wives, but at the time they were speaking, we did not have ears to hear. Why? We didn't have ears to hear because another voice had already captured our attention. Remember, when I stated earlier that the things which we are interested in, the words that capture our focus would be the things we listen to and move us.

Many of our wives are unusual in that they can watch a movie, check their emails, talk to the children on the phone, and crochet at the same time. Unfortunately, that is not the way men function. We are not hot-wired to do so much in the area of multitasking. It doesn't mean that we can't multitask; it just means that we need to be interested in each task. Many men, however, can't multitask. If we are watching a TV show, we must pause it to do anything else. For many of us, only one thing can capture our attention at a time. We are not unusual in this.

People as a whole believe they are good at multitasking. In a recent scientific study, however, the effects of multitasking on different parts of the brain concluded that many people are far worse than they imagined at accomplishing more than one thing at a time. In these tests, the scientists found that almost everyone, men and women, thought too highly of their multitasking abilities and achieved a sub-par score in the evidence. Knowing our limitations, we realize that if we want to hear the voice of God, our walk must be in such a way that we are aware of other inputs which distract us from hearing the Father's voice. God's voice needs to be more than just another background noise.

When we pick up a book to read, we approach it the way or method in which we have learned to read. We all approach reading differently. Some scan the text to see if it is worth the time and effort to invest the time to read. Some read the last chapter first to get over the suspense. Some scan the chapter titles and just read the sections that sound interesting. Some treat the Bible, God's voice, and God's presence the same way they read a book. They scan and try to pick and choose what they deem to be necessary.

When some of us read, we can be easily distracted. Sounds, shiny objects, and reflections in the window can easily distract us and draw us away from our reading. Since we are aware that we can be easily distracted, when the time comes to go into sincere prayer or intensive study of God's Word, we must go into our study room and shut out noises and distractions. However, retreating to the stillness and quietness of a room free from outside distractions will not settle the mind of all the internal disturbances of things we need to accomplish, places we need to go, something we need at the store, and phone calls and texts we need to return. Taking your phone into your quiet room will add to the frustration of not being able to focus your attention on hearing God and receiving the eternal things of the Kingdom.

The things I've listed that will be internal distractions from calming the mind need to be removed. We also need to remove the hinderances of hearing God. There is one distraction not covered yet, which we all will do battle. The voices that speak in the mind will remind us of our failures, disappointments, and broken promises with God. All of these are distractions to keep us in a failed position of hearing God's voice. By the way, if we believe the Scriptures, then we need to practice placing them into action.

1 Peter 5:7 ESV casting all your anxieties on him, because he cares for you.

The need to shut ourselves in and isolate ourselves from distractions is not necessary with some of us. When some people read or pray, they can have the house falling in around them, and they still would be soaring through page after page or engaged in deep intercession. They have ears for what they are reading and can easily tune out everything else. For some of us, we know that if we desire to hear from the Father, we certainly must rid any distractions which would draw us away from God's voice and do as our Lord did and retreat to the mountains.

There needs to be within each of us, a longing, desire, and ability to recognize God's Word when He speaks. Some of the best news we can have today is that God is speaking to us. Because the Father is speaking, He wants us to become so familiar with His voice that all He needs to do is whisper our name, and we say, "Yes, Lord." Relationships deepen through fellowship. The more time we spend in association with the Father, the more we will act like, think like, and talk like a son of the King, and the clearer the Father's voice becomes to us.

God wants us to hear Him. He is not holding back His voice from us. We are the ones who need to decide to listen and then follow through with the necessary actions to meet with the Father. We need to position ourselves to hear from the Father.

> *Jeremiah 29:11-13 ESV For I know the plans I have for you, declares the LORD, plans for welfare and not for evil, to give you a future and a hope. (12) Then you will call upon me and come and pray to me, and I will hear you. (13) You will seek me and find me, when you seek me with all your heart.*
>
> *Jude 1:21 ESV keep yourselves in the love of God, waiting for the mercy of our Lord Jesus Christ that leads to eternal life.*

Suppose it is raining outside. It is summertime and one of those inviting rains that seem to scream to us, "come out and take a walk in the rain." We must decide if we want to leave the dry, comfortable surroundings of our home to go out and position ourselves under the refreshing drops of the rainfall. We do not have to tell children to have fun in the rain. As we age, we might forget those simple things that once brought so much joy and lasting memories. Why do we lose the memories of those things that we once enjoyed so much as children? The pleasure of stomping in the rain puddles as children become nothing more than a nuisance as an adult.

It is the same as being a believer. We can witness more young Christians talking about hearing the Father speaking to them than from the senior believers. It would seem that as we get older in years as a Christian, we have learned to position ourselves under the umbrella out of the rain, meaning that sometimes we get too practical, smart, and comfortable to hear God's voice. The opposite should be true. As we add years to our Christian life, we should be more accustomed to hearing God's voice and more aggressive to get in on what God is doing.

> *Matthew 18:3 ESV and said, "Truly, I say to you, unless you turn and become like children, you will never enter the kingdom of heaven.*
>
> *Mark 10:15 ESV Truly, I say to you, whoever does not receive the kingdom of God like a child shall not enter it."*

HEARING GOD'S VOICE CARRIES WITH IT A GREAT RESPONSIBILITY ON THE HEARER

Imagine if we could hear God the Father with full assurance that it was His voice. Our job in the hearing process is to develop and have ears that long to hear from the Father. It would be a good reminder for our readers that God does not just speak for the sake of talking. He wants us to hear with the intent to obey. Having this intent to follow is having an open and willing heart. If we had ears to listen to the still small voice of the Father as we should, we would walk each day in His confidence. We would also treat our spouse and children differently, and we would walk in our vocations without doubt or fear.

In ministry times, many say that they want to hear God and know what God has for them. There is one thing about "saying" that we want to hear and understand, and another thing to live with a heart to listen to, receive and obey what the Father is saying. Those who cry out, "I want to hear God," need to understand that it is not God holding back His voice. He is not in heaven, silent and pouting. He is speaking because He is a loving and caring Father that desires for us to come into the full measure of our faith.

We all know people who carry opinions about how we should live our lives and what we should believe about God. We all have individuals who have expressed their views about what we should believe, how and what should be preached and taught, and how we should relate to others. The emotion drives much of this without any thoughts about what God says in His Word.

We all have had the joy of knowing and relating to people who have great ideas and opinions about us. There is only one opinion that should matter to us, and that is the viewpoint of our heavenly Father. What if we cried out to the Father to search our hearts and try our thoughts, yet we never positioned ourselves to hear His voice? How can we see what the Father sees and know what the Father knows if we don't have ears to hear and eyes to see?

> *Psalms 139:23-24 ESV Search me, O God, and know my heart! Try me and know my thoughts! (24) And see if there be any grievous way in me, and lead me in the way everlasting!*

If God's opinion about us matters, then it would stand to reason that hearing His voice over all other views should be a top priority for us. Once we get a specific word from the Lord, we set our face like a flint and become focused on His will and desire for our lives.

> *Isaiah 50:7 ESV But the Lord GOD helps me; therefore I have not been disgraced; therefore I have set my face like a flint, and I know that I shall not be put to shame.*

10

KEYS TO UNLOCKING THE TREASURE OF GOD'S VOICE

In this chapter, I want to give the 15 different ways to hear the voice of God and the four straightforward keys to unlocking the treasure of God's voice. I will not get into the details of the 15 ways of hearing God's voice. The second book of this series, "So, You Want To Hear God's Voice?" will cover in detail the 15 ways to hear. I don't presume to know everything about hearing the voice of God, nor do I want to declare that there are only 15 ways to hear God's voice. I will update this material as God reveals from His written Word new ways of hearing His voice. I can say, however, that these 15 ways of understanding the voice of God are spoken of and verified by a living example within the Word of God.

I do not believe that we should have an experience or particular mindset, (system of personal beliefs), and then attempt to force the Scriptures, (even if it means Scripture twisting or taking Scriptures out of context), to validate the experiences or beliefs. I believe that the only accurate way of Scripture interpretation is to bring the expertise or mindset under the heavy scrutiny of God's Word. If the experience does not line up with Scripture, then the experience is under question, not the Word of God.

Here are the 15 ways to hear God. Again, you can divide some of these and come up with 20 ideas to hear God's voice. But some are so close in function and method I decided to combine them. Again, the validating Scriptures and examples are in Book 2 of this series of "So, You Want To Hear God's Voice," and is entitled "The 15 Ways To Hear The Voice Of God.

1. The Holy Spirit,
2. The Bible,
3. Prayer and fasting,
4. Our Lord Jesus Christ,
5. Symbolic actions,
6. A gentle whisper,
7. Miraculous signs,
8. Prophets, preachers, teachers, speakers, and other people,
9. Media,
10. Circumstances,
11. Inner urges,
12. Dreams, visions and audible voices,
13. Nature,
14. Angles,
15. Ministry time,

These four keys are found in Habakkuk 2:1-2.

Habakkuk 2:1-3 ESV I will take my stand at my watchpost and station myself on the tower, and look out to see what he will say to me, and what I will answer concerning my complaint. (2) And the LORD answered me: "Write the vision; make it plain on tablets, so he may run who reads it. (3) For still the vision awaits its appointed time; it hastens to the end—it will not lie. If it seems slow, wait for it; it will surely come; it will not delay.

PREPARING OURSELVES TO HEAR GOD'S VOICE

Key #1: God's voice in our heart often sounds like a flow of spontaneous thoughts.

Habakkuk knew the sound of God speaking to him (See Hab.2:2). Elijah described it as a still, small voice (See I Kings 19:12). I had always listened to an inner audible voice, and God does speak that way at times. However, I have found that usually, God's voice comes as spontaneous thoughts, visions, feelings, or impressions.

For example, have you ever drove down the road and had an immediate impression of praying for a particular person? Didn't you believe it was God telling you to pray? What did God's voice sound like to you? Was it an audible voice, or was it a spontaneous thought that lit upon your mind? This thought is the same feeling when out of the blue, you get the incredible impression to call someone. You respond and make the call and find yourself ministering to a need. Did God initiate the feeling or idea to make the call? I believe so.

One definition of "paga," a Hebrew word for intercession, is "a chance encounter or an accidental intersecting." Don't be alarmed that I used the words "chance" or "accidental." It is not chance or accidental with God the Father. The Holy Spirit, which is always moving over the face of the Earth, speaks or guides us into "God's suddenlies." When God lays people on our heart, He does it through "paga." Now from our perspective it is a chance encounter or thought "accidentally" intersecting our minds. Therefore, when you want to hear from God, tune into a chance encounter of spontaneous thoughts, which is the moving of God's Spirit.

Key #2: Become still so you can sense God's flow of

thoughts and emotions within.

Habakkuk said, "I will stand on my guard post" (See Hab.2:1). Habakkuk knew that for someone to hear God's quiet, inner, spontaneous thoughts, he had to first go to a quiet place and still his thoughts and emotions.

> *Psalms 46:10 ESV "Be still, and know that I am God. I will be exalted among the nations, I will be exalted in the earth!"*

When we quiet our flesh and mind, we can experience a deep inner spontaneous flow of God's Holy Spirit in our spirit. If we are not still, we will sense only our thoughts. Loving God through a quiet song is one very effective way to become motionless before God. (See II Kings 3:15). After I praise or worship and become silent within, I open myself for that spontaneous flow of God's Spirit and God's Word. If thoughts come of things I have forgotten to do or need to do, I write them down and dismiss them. If feelings of guilt or unworthiness come, I immediately confess and repent completely, receive the washing of the blood of the Lamb, putting on His robe of righteousness, and seeing myself spotless before God, then I move on.

> *Isaiah 61:10 ESV I will greatly rejoice in the LORD; my soul shall exult in my God, for he has clothed me with the garments of salvation; he has covered me with the robe of righteousness, as a bridegroom decks himself like a priest with a beautiful headdress, and as a bride adorns herself with her jewels.*

> *Colossians 1:21-22 ESV And you, who once were alienated and hostile in mind, doing evil deeds, (22)*

> *he has now reconciled in his body of flesh by his death, in order to present you holy and blameless and above reproach before him,*

Our hearts must be focused appropriately upon God to receive the pure Word of God. If we fix our eyes upon our Lord Jesus Christ, the flow of His Holy Spirit comes. However, if we set our gaze upon a desire flowing from our own heart, we fulfill the lust of the flesh. To have a genuine move of God's Spirit, we must become still and carefully fix our eyes upon the Lord Jesus Christ. Again, quietly worshiping the King and receiving out of the stillness, the move of His Spirit is our desire. Fixing our gaze on the Lord Jesus, becoming quiet in His presence, and sharing with Him what is in our heart, opens us up to hearing God's voice in different ways. Spontaneous thoughts as He speaks to us will begin to flow from the throne of God, and we will be conversing with the King of Kings.

> *Hebrews 12:2 ESV looking to Jesus, the founder and perfecter of our faith, who for the joy that was set before him endured the cross, despising the shame, and is seated at the right hand of the throne of God.*

Key #3: As you pray, fix the eyes of your heart upon the Lord Jesus Christ and see in the spirit the dreams and visions of Almighty God.

We are spirit, soul, and body. We are a spirit, and we have a soul our thoughts (our mind), our feelings (our emotions), and we have our choices (our will). So, we are a spirit, we have a soul, and our body contains both. Our physical body traps the real us. It is essential to remember that when we look in the mirror, we are not seeing us, but only a shell that contains our spirit and soul. The supernatural, the kingdom of God, is in the spiritual realm. We spend to much time and resources on the temporal fleshly realm. God is a Spirit, and those who worship Him must worship Him in Spirit and truth.

> *John 4:24 ESV God is spirit, and those who worship him must worship in spirit and truth."*

Habakkuk said, "I will keep watch to see," And God said, "Record the vision" (See Hab.2:1-2). Habakkuk was looking for a vision as he prayed. He opened the eyes of his heart and looked into the spirit world to see what God wanted to show him. Seeing God's plan is an intriguing idea. God has always spoken through dreams and visions, and He specifically said that these would come to those upon whom the Holy Spirit is poured out.

> *Acts 2:16-17 ESV But this is what was uttered through the prophet Joel: (17) "'And in the last days it shall be, God declares, that I will pour out my Spirit on all flesh, and your sons and your daughters shall prophesy, and your young men shall see visions, and your old men shall dream dreams;*

In times past, I never thought of opening the eyes of my heart and looking for a vision from heaven. In retrospect, I have come to believe that opening the eyes of my heart is precisely what God wants me to do. He gave me eyes in my heart to see in the Spirit the vision and movement of Almighty God. He wants us to live with the expectation and desire that we will meet with Him. There is an active spirit world all around us, full of angels, demons, the Holy Spirit, the omnipresent Father, and His omnipresent Son, the Lord

Jesus Christ. The only reasons for me not seeing this reality would be unbelief, lack of knowledge, lack of expectation, or fixing my gaze on the natural and temporal things of this world.

To see, we must look. Daniel saw a vision in his mind and said, "I was looking, I kept looking, and I kept looking." When Daniel looked again, his vision scene would change. So, when you have a vision, don't get so excited and in a hurry that you run off. Keep looking for the complete picture that God wants to give. I have underlined certain words in the text below. These highlighted words communicate the literal meaning that Daniel looked again and then again into the vision of God.

> *Daniel 7:1-21 ESV In the first year of Belshazzar king of Babylon, Daniel saw a dream and visions of his head as he lay in his bed. Then he wrote down the dream and told the sum of the matter. (2) Daniel declared, "__I saw__ in my vision by night, and behold, the four winds of heaven were stirring up the great sea. (3) And four great beasts came up out of the sea, different from one another. (4) The first was like a lion and had eagles' wings. Then __as I looked__ its wings were plucked off, and it was lifted up from the ground and made to stand on two feet like a man, and the mind of a man was given to it. (5) And behold, another beast, a second one, like a bear. It was raised up on one side. It had three ribs in its mouth between its teeth; and it was told, 'Arise, devour much flesh.' (6) After this __I looked,__ and behold, another, like a leopard, with four wings of a bird on its back. And the beast had four heads, and dominion was given to it. (7) After this __I saw__ in the night visions, and*

behold, a fourth beast, terrifying and dreadful and exceedingly strong. It had great iron teeth; it devoured and broke in pieces and stamped what was left with its feet. It was different from all the beasts that were before it, and it had ten horns. (8) **I considered** the horns, and behold, there came up among them another horn, a little one, before which three of the first horns were plucked up by the roots. And behold, in this horn were eyes like the eyes of a man, and a mouth speaking great things. (9) "**As I looked**, thrones were placed, and the Ancient of Days took his seat; his clothing was white as snow, and the hair of his head like pure wool; his throne was fiery flames; its wheels were burning fire. (10) A stream of fire issued and came out from before him; a thousand thousands served him, and ten thousand times ten thousand stood before him; the court sat in judgment, and the books were opened. (11) "**I looked** then because of the sound of the great words that the horn was speaking. And **as I looked**, the beast was killed, and its body destroyed and given over to be burned with fire. (12) As for the rest of the beasts, their dominion was taken away, but their lives were prolonged for a season and a time. (13) "**I saw** in the night visions, and behold, with the clouds of heaven **there came** one like a son of man, and he came to the Ancient of Days and was presented before him. (14) And to him was given dominion and glory and a kingdom, that all peoples, nations, and languages should serve him; his dominion is an everlasting dominion, which shall not pass away, and his kingdom one that shall not be destroyed. (15) "As for me, Daniel, my spirit within me was anxious,

> *and the visions of my head alarmed me. (16) I approached one of those who stood there and asked him the truth concerning all this. So he told me and made known to me the interpretation of the things. (17) 'These four great beasts are four kings who shall arise out of the earth. (18) But the saints of the Most High shall receive the kingdom and possess the kingdom forever, forever and ever.' (19) "Then I desired to know the truth about the fourth beast, which was different from all the rest, exceedingly terrifying, with its teeth of iron and claws of bronze, and which devoured and broke in pieces and stamped what was left with its feet, (20) and about the ten horns that were on its head, and the other horn that came up and before which three of them fell, the horn that had eyes and a mouth that spoke great things, and that seemed greater than its companions. (21) **<u>As I looked</u>**, this horn made war with the saints and prevailed over them,*

As we pray, we should be watching as our Lord Jesus Christ speaks to us, doing and saying the things that are in His heart. Many Christians will find that if they only look, they will see in the same way they receive spontaneous thoughts. Jesus is Emmanuel, (Immanuel), God with us (See Matt.1:23). It is as simple as that. We can see Christ present with us because Christ is present with us. The vision may come so smoothly it could tempt us to reject it, thinking that it is just us, or the pizza we ate. Conversely, if we persist in recording these visions, our doubts will soon be overcome by faith, and we will recognize that the content of the images and dreams could only be birthed in us by Almighty God.

Our Lord Jesus Christ demonstrated the ability to live from a place of constant contact with the Father. He declared that He did nothing on His initiative, but only what He saw the Father doing and heard the Father saying.

> *John 5:19-20 ESV So Jesus said to them, "Truly, truly, I say to you, the Son can do nothing of his own accord, but only what he sees the Father doing. For whatever the Father does, that the Son does likewise. (20) For the Father loves the Son and shows him all that he himself is doing. And greater works than these will he show him, so that you may marvel.*

> *John 5:30 ESV "I can do nothing on my own. As I hear, I judge, and my judgment is just, because I seek not my own will but the will of him who sent me.*

What an incredible way to live! Is it possible for us to live out of divine initiative as our Lord Jesus Christ did? I believe that the answer is a resounding, "Yes." Our Lord Jesus Christ Himself said that we would do the things that He did and even more because He goes to the Father. This life of faith comes as we learn to fix our eyes on Jesus.

We, as believers, no longer need to fix our eyes on the cross. The finished work of the cross by our Lord declared salvation to all who would come. Before you panic, let me say that the cross is first and foremost. There is no salvation except through the work of the cross. But what do we need after we've been to the cross? God said that when we need to come boldly before the throne of grace. He did not tell us to go back to the cross. We have been there. We have appropriated what we needed to settle our sin nature issue. Now we stand before the throne to ask and to receive. The temple veil, torn from top to bottom, gives us access into the immediate presence of God, and He calls us to draw near. "My prayer is that the eyes of our heart will be enlightened..."

> *John 14:12 ESV "Truly, truly, I say to you, whoever believes in me will also do the works that I do; and greater works than these will he do, because I am going to the Father.*
>
> *Luke 23:44-45 ESV It was now about the sixth hour, and there was darkness over the whole land until the ninth hour, (45) while the sun's light failed. And the curtain of the temple was torn in two.*
>
> *Hebrews 4:15-16 ESV For we do not have a high priest who is unable to sympathize with our weaknesses, but one who in every respect has been tempted as we are, yet without sin. (16) Let us then with confidence draw near to the throne of grace, that we may receive mercy and find grace to help in time of need.*
>
> *Hebrews 10:18-22 ESV Where there is forgiveness of these, there is no longer any offering for sin. (19) Therefore, brothers, since we have confidence to enter the holy places by the blood of Jesus, (20) by the new and living way that he opened for us through the curtain, that is, through his flesh, (21) and since we have a great priest over the house of God, (22) let us draw near with a true heart in full assurance of faith, with our hearts sprinkled clean from an evil conscience and our bodies washed with pure water.*
>
> *Ephesians 1:16-19 ESV I do not cease to give thanks for you, remembering you in my prayers, (17) that the God of our Lord Jesus Christ, the Father of glory,*

> *may give you the Spirit of wisdom and of revelation in the knowledge of him, (18) having the eyes of your hearts enlightened, that you may know what is the hope to which he has called you, what are the riches of his glorious inheritance in the saints, (19) and what is the immeasurable greatness of his power toward us who believe, according to the working of his great might*

Key #4: Journaling, the writing out of your prayers, God's answers, and impressions, brings great freedom in hearing God's voice.

God told Habakkuk to record the vision (See Hab.2:2). This command from God was not an isolated command. The Scriptures record many examples of individual prayers, God's replies, and impressions. Cases would be such as in the Psalms, many of the Prophets, and the Book of Revelation. We can call this process, "two-way journaling." As I journal, I can write in faith for long periods, simply believing it is God. These words eventually become material for books for the body of Christ.

I know that the testing of the words which I believe I have received from God is a must. I don't want to test them while I am trying to collect them. I will check it after I receive it. With journaling, I can receive in faith, knowing that when the flow of what I believe to be God's Spirit speaking to me has ended, I can test and scrutinize it against two things, the Word of God and the character of God. This testing is making sure that it lines up with Scripture and the Character of the Father. You will be amazed when you journal. Doubt may hinder you at first but throw it off, reminding yourself that hearing God is a biblical concept and that God is always present, speaking to His children.

Relax. When we cease our labors and enter His rest, God is free to flow by His Spirit.

> *Hebrews 4:9-11 ESV So then, there remains a Sabbath rest for the people of God, (10) for whoever has entered God's rest has also rested from his works as God did from his. (11) Let us therefore strive to enter that rest, so that no one may fall by the same sort of disobedience.*

Sit back comfortably, turn off your phone, take out your pen and paper, your Bible, smile, and turn your attention toward the Lord in praise and worship while seeking His face. After you write your question to Him, become still while fixing your gaze on the Lord Jesus Christ. You will suddenly have an excellent thought from the person of the Holy Spirit. Don't doubt it; simply write it down. Later, as you read your journaling, you will be blessed to discover that you are indeed conversing with the Father.

Knowing God through the Bible is a vital foundation for hearing His voice in your heart. Therefore, you must have a substantial commitment to understanding and obeying the Scriptures. It is also imperative for your growth and safety that you be related to trustworthy spiritual leaders. All the main directional moves that come through journaling, such as relocating, vocational changes, significant financial commitments, engagement, or marriage decisions, should have confirmation by your leaders or the prophets of the ministry that you are associated with before you act upon them. This confirmation is not about control, but to ensure you are correctly hearing from the Father and not being deceived by the desire of your emotions.

Proverbs 15:22 ESV Without counsel plans fail, but with many advisers they succeed.

Proverbs 11:14 ESV Where there is no guidance, a people falls, but in an abundance of counselors there is safety.

11

THINGS TO REMEMBER AS YOU SEEK TO HEAR GOD'S VOICE

We spoke about getting ourselves prepared to listen to God. We mentioned the many ways that God speaks to us. We talked about the four keys to unlocking God's voice in our lives. All of this is paramount. But remember this: The "how God speaks" is not nearly as important as the fact that He speaks and what He says. Some run from one prophetic meeting to another prophetic meeting to get "a word from the Lord." To some people, getting a word becomes an "end in itself." They lack the resolve and conviction to follow through with obedience to the instruction given.

NO POINT OF REFERENCE, NO PRECEDENT, ONLY THE WORD OF GOD

I will attempt to summarize all that we have said before using a Biblical example. As we reflected on one such occasion when God spoke to Moses, I want us to note four essential facts about the way God speaks. We will look at God speaking to Moses in the third chapter of Genesis. What? Did God talk to Moses in Genesis 3? Isn't Genesis 3 about Adam and Eve and their sin and rebellion, and the Book of Exodus about Moses? True! However, God spoke this historical account to Moses hundreds of years later to record it for our benefit.

Moses, as he began to write, had no point of reference

to how all creation started except through the revelation of God speaking to him and the oral tradition of the passing of the stories from one generation to another. But where did each person get that oral tradition? Each incredible accurate tale of those before Moses had to start with someone who had an encounter with God. The Father did so by relating these facts directly to Moses by way of the Holy Spirit.

When God speaks, it is usually unique to that individual. Moses had no precedent for a burning bush experience. He couldn't look back at history and draw from someone else's encounter with God. This experience was new to him and new to anyone else. There were no books out on the market about having a burning bush experience, which would cause Moses to be waiting for his time to experience this. He couldn't say, "Oh, finally, this is my burning bush experience."

Abraham had his experience of meeting with God. God had not demanded a human sacrifice before, so Abraham was standing in faith that he heard God correctly. In Hebrews chapter 11, it states that Abraham believed that he was going to kill his son Isaac and God was going to raise him from the dead. Where did Abraham get such an idea of the resurrection from the dead? There was no precedent yet from which he could draw that knowledge. God spoke, and the Scriptures say that Abraham believed God and obeyed, and it was accounted to him righteousness.

Isaac had his own experience of meeting with God, and Jacob had his unique encounter, and now I get to experience my own. What about Noah building an ark because God told him there was going to rain a flood that would cover the earth. It had not rained yet, so Noah had no point of reference, yet he believed God and built an ark in the middle of the desert away from the river.

Moses' experience was unique. Man tends to copy the familiar, and yet the Father wants our encounter with Him and His voice to us to be personal and exclusive to us. We may not know how it will happen or what it will look like, but we can trust God that our experiences with Him will happen, just because God is God.

If Moses was alive and preaching today, the temptation might drive him to write a book called, "My Burning Bush Experience: 10 Easy Steps of How You Can Have One Too!" Many believers would be reading it, traveling out to desert places, and looking for their "burning bush" experience. We must not become distracted on imitating the experiences of people mentioned in the Bible, but instead, learn that God did speak, and He still speaks to His children today. This example does not mean that what God did in the Bible He won't do today, because He is God and can repeat past experiences. If you are quick to defend that God wants to repeat past experiences, then I want to know how many times you have walked on water and how many people you know that have walked on water. It's not that it can't happen when the Lord calls us out of the boat, but there must be a lesson where we build faith up, and the Father glorified. In other words, God is not going to let anyone walk on water just for the emotional rush of doing something unique and "cool."

James 4:3 ESV You ask and do not receive, because you ask wrongly, to spend it on your passions.

When God speaks, we can take steps to be sure it is God talking. The Scripture tells us that when God spoke to Moses through the burning bush, he had no question about the fact that God was the one speaking. Likewise, we can recognize the voice of God.

> *John 10:4-5 ESV When he has brought out all his own, he goes before them, and the sheep follow him, for they know his voice. (5) A stranger they will not follow, but they will flee from him, for they do not know the voice of strangers."*

If I have trouble hearing God's voice, then I either do not belong to God, or I am not right with God! In Lk.11:33-36, our Lord Jesus speaks about the key to spiritual perception. Our Lord had just talked about the spiritual blindness of His generation (See Lk.11:29-32). Now our Lord Jesus speaks to the question of whose fault it is when there is a lack of spiritual perception. In so doing, He teaches us that the key to spiritual understanding is a pure heart.

> *Luke 11:33-36 ESV "No one after lighting a lamp puts it in a cellar or under a basket, but on a stand, so that those who enter may see the light. (34) Your eye is the lamp of your body. When your eye is healthy, your whole body is full of light, but when it is bad, your body is full of darkness. (35) Therefore be careful lest the light in you be darkness. (36) If then your whole body is full of light, having no part dark, it will be wholly bright, as when a lamp with its rays gives you light."*

> *Matthew 5:8 ESV "Blessed are the pure in heart, for they shall see God.*

Lack of spiritual perception is not God's fault (See Lk.11:33). One of the purposes of light is to help one find his way in the dark. Therefore, in lighting a darkened room, one will place his lamp on a location of prominence such as a lampstand so that it might provide as much light as possible. The point here is that God works to reveal Himself to us. Lack of spiritual perception falls totally on us as our responsibility (See Lk.11:34-36).

Our Lord Jesus tells us that our eyes work to help us when we maneuver. By deciphering the various images of light that bombard them, our eyes help us know how to get about in this world. If our eyes are damaged or diseased, then everything goes dark, and we are left to stumble and fall. He then goes on to speak of one's heart, "the light within you" (See Lk.11:35), as is the organ by which we discern spiritual light. If our hearts have become darkened, then we are left without spiritual perception and condemned to wander in spiritual darkness. Paul speaks of this in Ephesians 4:18.

> *Ephesians 4:17-19 ESV Now this I say and testify in the Lord, that you must no longer walk as the Gentiles do, in the futility of their minds. (18) They are darkened in their understanding, alienated from the life of God because of the ignorance that is in them, due to their hardness of heart. (19) They have become callous and have given themselves up to sensuality, greedy to practice every kind of impurity.*

How does this hardness develop? It develops from time after time of choosing not to walk in the light we have received. God has taken a natural law that we know from farming and has established a spiritual law in the universe, which governs a man's well-being.

> *Galatians 6:7-9 ESV Do not be deceived: God is not mocked, for whatever one sows, that will he also*

> *reap. (8) For the one who sows to his own flesh will from the flesh reap corruption, but the one who sows to the Spirit will from the Spirit reap eternal life. (9) And let us not grow weary of doing good, for in due season we will reap, if we do not give up.*

If one sows rejection of God's light, he will reap spiritual blindness; but if he sows reception of God's light, he will reap spiritual perception. If I am traveling in my car at night with my headlights on the low light beams, they will only shine so far in front of my car. However, they shine far enough to let me know where I am to go. When I have traveled the distance currently lit by my headlights, I find that they now shine much farther down the road to let me know where to go next. I can't outrun the light that is shining in front of me. It is the same with the guidance of God. We walk in the light He has given us today knowing that as we do, there will be even more light provided tomorrow, and we can't outrun the illumination of God.

When God speaks, we can understand what God is saying. It is not in the heart of the Father that we would stay in darkness, unaware of His will and ways. Moses knew what God wanted, how He wanted it done, and when He wanted it done. Likewise, we can understand what God wants us to do, how God wants it done, and when God wants it done.

> *Psalms 37:3-6 ESV Trust in the LORD, and do good; dwell in the land and befriend faithfulness. (4) Delight yourself in the LORD, and he will give you the desires of your heart. (5) Commit your way to the LORD; trust in him, and he will act. (6) He will bring forth your righteousness as the light, and your justice as the noonday.*

As we delight in the Lord, He will not only tell us what He wants us to do, (See Ps.37:4), but how our Lord wants it done and when He wants us to get started, (See Ps.37:5). When God speaks, we can discern His guidance. Too many believers are making decisions based on what they think God may have said. It is a hit and miss lifestyle driven by guesswork on what God may or may not have said. This guesswork is not the way the Father established to reveal His will and means to His children. As we are winding down the book, I want to give one more Scriptural example of hearing and acting on God's words from Acts 11:1-18.

> *Acts 11:1-18 ESV Now the apostles and the brothers who were throughout Judea heard that the Gentiles also had received the word of God. (2) So when Peter went up to Jerusalem, the circumcision party criticized him, saying, (3) "You went to uncircumcised men and ate with them." (4) But Peter began and explained it to them in order: (5) "I was in the city of Joppa praying, and in a trance I saw a vision, something like a great sheet descending, being let down from heaven by its four corners, and it came down to me. (6) Looking at it closely, I observed animals and beasts of prey and reptiles and birds of the air. (7) And I heard a voice saying to me, 'Rise, Peter; kill and eat.' (8) But I said, 'By no means, Lord; for nothing common or unclean has ever entered my mouth.' (9) But the voice answered a second time from heaven, 'What God has made clean, do not call common.' (10) This happened three times, and all was drawn up again into heaven. (11) And behold, at that very moment three men arrived at the house in*

which we were, sent to me from Caesarea. (12) And the Spirit told me to go with them, making no distinction. These six brothers also accompanied me, and we entered the man's house. (13) And he told us how he had seen the angel stand in his house and say, 'Send to Joppa and bring Simon who is called Peter; (14) he will declare to you a message by which you will be saved, you and all your household.' (15) As I began to speak, the Holy Spirit fell on them just as on us at the beginning. (16) And I remembered the word of the Lord, how he said, 'John baptized with water, but you will be baptized with the Holy Spirit.' (17) If then God gave the but you will be baptized with the Holy Spirit.' (17) If then God gave the same gift to them as he gave to us when we believed in the Lord Jesus Christ, who was I that I could stand in God's way?" (18) When they heard these things they fell silent. And they glorified God, saying, "Then to the Gentiles also God has granted repentance that leads to life."

There are six steps to hearing God's voice taken from Acts chapter 11.

Step #1: Spend time in communion with God: (See Acts 11:5)

Peter was taking time for prayer and meditation when God spoke to him. Likewise, if we would be in a position to hear God's voice and receive His direction, we must commit time to prayer and meditation in the presence of the Lord. Fasting is a useful tool to combine with prayer. When we do, we posture our hearts to hear from the Lord.

Step #2: Receive a personal vision from God: (See Acts 11:5)

Peter tells us that the language of the Holy Spirit is "dreams and visions" (See Acts 2:17). God implanted in Peter's heart (See Ps.37:4; Prov.29:18). We should also desire for God to speak to us through visions and dreams. Through applying steps one and two, God can implant in my heart a vision for WHAT He wants me to do. Through using the next four steps, I can then discern HOW and WHEN He wants me to do it.

Step #3: Look for opportunities given by God: (See Acts 11:11)

The late evangelist Steve Hill used to say that "we should seize the opportunity while there was an opportunity to be seized."

Step #4: Listen to the voice of the Spirit of God: (See Acts 11:12)

> *Colossians 3:15 ESV And let the peace of Christ rule in your hearts, to which indeed you were called in one body. And be thankful.*

> *1 Corinthians 14:33 ESV (33) For God is not a God of confusion but of peace. As in all the churches of the saints,*

Step #5: Enlist advice from Godly men and women: (See Acts 11:12)

> *Proverbs 11:14 ESV Where there is no guidance, a*

people falls, but in an abundance of counselors there is safety.

Proverbs 15:22 ESV Without counsel plans fail, but with many advisers, they succeed.

Step #6: Consider the testimony of the Word of God and the Character of God: (See Acts 11:16)

God's will can NEVER contradict His Word or His Character. God's Word and God's Character ALWAYS clarifies God's will and ways. When God speaks, we have an encounter with God. Moses would have been foolish to say, "This has been a wonderful experience speaking with this burning bush. I hope it leads to an encounter with God." It already was an encounter with God. Likewise, when God speaks to us, we may not yet know all that He has in mind. We may not know the how and the when of what we are to do. We may need to wait on Him further to discern His leadership, but we can rejoice in the fact that we have a Word from God and an encounter with our heavenly Father.

Conclusion:

In Hebrews 1:2, the Bible tells us that God has spoken by His Son and Jn.14:16-18 tells us that He still speaks by His Son, who abides within us by His Spirit. Today God speaks by His Spirit in many different ways as I have briefly listed in this book the 15 ways God speaks. I go into great detail in book 2, "15 Ways To Hear The Voice Of God." In closing, I want to remind us of these five key points:

> ➢ God has a personal word for each of us.

- When God speaks, we can be sure it is God speaking.
- When God speaks, we can know what God is saying.
- When God speaks, we can discern His guidance.
- When God speaks, that is an encounter with God Himself.

The Holy Spirit gives clear directives today. God is our personal, loving Father who wants to be intimately involved in our life. He will provide us with clear guidance for living a successful daily life. We may say, "That has not been my experience." I would tell you that you need to base your understanding of God on Scripture and not on experience or lack of experience. Hebrews 1:2 tells us that in times past, God spoke in various ways. Indeed, in the Old Testament we find that God spoke through angels, (See Gen.16:11-12), through visions, (See Gen.15:1), and through dreams, (See Gen.28:10-19).

So, there you have it, a book on how to prepare to hear God speak. He does want to talk to us if we're going to listen, (hearken-hear with the intent to obey). We must expect God to speak to us and to guide us as a typical Christian experience. We should have faith that He'll give us clear direction, and He surely will.

Psalms 32:8 ESV I will instruct you and teach you in the way you should go; I will counsel you with my eye upon you.

Make this golden pattern a part of your daily life!

Hearing God's voice is as simple as quieting yourself down, fixing your eyes on the Lord Jesus Christ, tuning in to spontaneity, and writing down what the Father is saying.

Closing prayer:

Lord, bless and anoint your church as they follow this Biblical pattern. Lord, we thank You for examples in Your Word which instruct our lives. Thank You for teaching so many of your children to hear Your voice in recent years. You are restoring our lives. You are a wonderful counselor. We worship You. To God, be glory forever and ever. Amen!

I hope this book has helped and will continue to help in your quest to know God's voice. May your knowledge increase in the way the Father works, and may you walk in greater intimacy with Him. We, the incredibly blessed people of God, can rejoice over the heavenly invitation to have ongoing conversations with Almighty God. He is the Creator of the Universe, the Creator of this world. Our loving Father is calling us into deep fellowship and intimacy with Him.

His sheep hear His voice and follow Him.

John 10:3-6 ESV To him the gatekeeper opens. The sheep hear his voice, and he calls his own sheep by name and leads them out. (4) When he has brought out all his own, he goes before them, and the sheep follow him, for they know his voice. (5) A stranger they will not follow, but they will flee from him, for they do not know the voice of strangers

PREPARING OURSELVES TO HEAR GOD'S VOICE

Made in the USA
Monee, IL
20 November 2020